Happy Indoor Garden

First published in the United Kingdom in 2023 by
B.T. Batsford Ltd
43 Great Ormond Street
London WC1N 3HZ
An imprint of
B.T. Batsford Holdings Ltd

ISBN 9781849948265

A CIP catalogue record for this book is available from the British Library.

30 29 28 27 26 25 24 23
10 9 8 7 6 5 4 3 2 1

Reproduction by Rival Colour Ltd, UK
Printed by Toppan Leefung Ltd, China

This book can be ordered direct from the publisher at www.batsford.com.

Happy Indoor Garden

Miranda Janatka

BATSFORD

Contents

Introduction

Thriving houseplants can do more for our homes than artwork, furniture or any other stylish and decorative items. Plants actually have a long history of being brought inside to improve surroundings, both aesthetically and for well-being. There is even evidence that the Ancient Greeks, Egyptians and many other early civilizations, enjoyed having plants in their homes as well as other indoor spaces. In recent years, a resurgence in popularity has resulted in houseplants once again being used more widely, with a broader range available than ever before to suit many individual tastes and budgets.

However, plants that are suffering have precisely the opposite effect on rooms and the people inside them. They look awful, make us miserable, and can also be a huge waste of money. Without knowing how to care for the plants you buy, as well as where to keep them, your plants won't stay healthy and beautiful for long. This book provides information on how to care for, and where to grow, 25 of the most popular and useful houseplants, plus many more throughout the book, making indoor gardening an easy and joyful experience.

Each room in a home provides its own challenges and opportunities for growing creatively and successfully. We'll explore the main rooms in turn, providing you with an expert eye and feel for what works. This is perfect for using alongside other interior design ideas and ensuring you choose the right plant to thrive in every space. Where a room is not specifically mentioned by name, the information included here will enable you to assess its conditions and match it closely to another one described. There are 20 specific design ideas detailed in this book, and over 150 plants suggested throughout, to set you up for success with a wide range of options.

Use the second half of the book for guidance and inspiration – find plants that you may already own and improve the way you care for them. Then use it as a catalogue and choose the new ones you want to buy, ready to ensure they'll flourish once you have them home. The plants have been selected as some of the most beautiful, easy to source and care for.

Whether you're redecorating your home, planning seasonal changes or just want to add some personal touches to a space you're renting, this book will inspire and inform. It distils years of horticultural knowledge and professional experience down to the fundamental information you need to grow houseplants. When they're happy, plants provide interest, conversation starters, organic form and sometimes even some visual 'wow'-factor. Happy plants make for stylish, joyful homes and this book will demystify the secrets of successful growing to reveal the palette of greenery that awaits you.

The Fundamentals

Houseplants need light, heat, air, water and nutrients to grow. While different plants require different amounts of each element, they all need the right quantity of each to remain healthy. For example, providing a plant with plenty of warmth and light, but not enough (or too much) water will mean that it'll struggle to grow well. Water is needed as part of photosynthesis, but also to help regulate temperature and move nutrients around the plant. If a plant is surrounded by more water than it can absorb for too long, its roots will rot and it will lose the ability to take up any moisture at all.

We can look to nature to best understand the needs of our plants. Those that grow on shady jungle floors will have spent thousands of years evolving to optimize growth in that particular environment. They simply cannot cope with much more or much less heat, water, certain nutrients or light than they would receive in their natural environment. The following section provides information to help understand the needs of your plants as well as the conditions of any room you plan to grow them in.

Light

Plants use certain wavelengths of light, alongside carbon dioxide, water and chlorophyll to photosynthesize, which is how they make energy to live and grow. The most useful wavelengths for this are in the blue and red range, found naturally in sunlight. Chlorophyll can be seen as the green pigment in various plant parts and enables them to absorb light. The larger the area of green (typically the leaves) and the deeper the colour, the more chlorophyll is present. Variegated plants need more light to photosynthesize than those with big, deep green leaves. For a room with less natural sunlight, choose a plant with lots of green foliage so it can better capture and make more efficient use of the available light.

If you live in the Northern Hemisphere, the strongest light coming into your home will be through south-facing windows, with the least coming from the north. Those living in the Southern Hemisphere can reverse this, but all parts of the world can expect more light in the morning through their east-facing windows, and more in the evening through their west. Obviously, daylight hours are also longer everywhere during the summer months.

The different types of light found indoors can be referred to as low light, partial shade, indirect bright light and bright light. Most plants, except cacti and succulents, will thrive with indirect bright light. This is usually an area that is well-lit but out of danger of being scorched by strong light, such as around – but not directly in front of – a window. Bear in mind that light levels change throughout the day, year, and according to the weather outside, but you can use this as a starting point. The diagram adjacent shows where you would likely find the different types of light in a room.

Rooms with lower light levels can benefit from paler walls and mirrors to reflect light, as well as the use of supplementary lighting. While standard lights inside homes do not provide enough red and blue wavelengths for photosynthesis, specialized LED grow lights can provide a broader spectrum of light, and it is now possible to buy ones that are indistinguishable from standard home bulbs (only a warm white or yellow glow is visible). Although they are becoming more widely available, they sometimes need adapters, so check the instructions. Also, remember that plants will grow in the direction of growth-supporting light. Up-lighting from the floor may be attractive but could make for wonky plants. (See pp.42–43 for using LED lights.)

Areas where you would typically find different types of light in a room are
1) Bright light, 2) Indirect bright light, 3) Partial shade, 4) Low light

Temperature and humidity

Most houseplants generally enjoy a daytime temperature of around 18–24°C (64–75°F) and a night-time temperature of around 15–20°C (59–68°F). A drop in temperature between seasons will benefit many plants as they will rest in response to this, and in some cases go dormant, providing more energy for growth and new flowers the following year.

Relative humidity in most rooms of the home ranges between 30–60 per cent, depending on various factors which we will explore in the book. Two types of humidity are generally discussed: absolute humidity, which is the actual amount of water vapour present in the air; and relative humidity, which is the ratio of the amount of water vapour in the air at a given temperature. For growing houseplants, we are interested in relative humidity as it tells us how much water vapour is in the air, compared to how much there could be at the same temperature. Relative humidity of 10 per cent we know is low, whereas 90 per cent, which you might find in a bathroom after a shower, is very wet air. The warmer the air, the more moisture it can hold, which is why we consider heat and moisture at the same time. Unfortunately, hot air such as the air found next to a radiator can draw moisture out of a plant and therefore the plant will need more regular watering. Conversely, in a particularly cold room, compost in a pot can remain wet for longer, which is not great for succulents.

It is possible to buy home thermometers that can also tell you the relative humidity of a room. Alternatively, observe how your plants respond to their environment. The leaves of plants in a room with not enough humidity may turn crispy and brown at the ends or have buds that fall off before flowering. Plants in a room with too much humidity will rot, much in the same way as when they don't have the opportunity to dry out between waterings.

Your kitchen, bathroom, utility room or anywhere else that creates heat, uses water and is enclosed, is likely to have a higher temperature and relative humidity than areas that are open to the outdoors and unheated. If humidity is too low for your plants, group them together – this enables them to support one another with moisture evaporating from their leaves. Misting and placing plant pots on top of trays of water are other ways to increase humidity, but with a limited or temporary effect. Ultimately, the best way to grow plants that enjoy high humidity in a room with low humidity is to grow them in a terrarium. See pp.40–41 for more information.

Small thermometers that also display relative humidity can be tucked neatly beside or behind plants.

Watering and feeding

Watering houseplants can be tricky. A plant growing in the ground or in the branches of a tree will benefit from excess moisture being able to drain away. However, by growing a plant in a pot, it's possible for the plant to sit wet for too long. But, it can also become too dry as it relies solely on you watering it. Check the compost before and in between waterings by sticking your finger at least 1cm (½in) into the soil to check if it is wet. Lift the pot out of its decorative cover pot occasionally to check it isn't sitting in a pool of water and to see if the roots are growing out of the pot and the plant requires repotting. A plant overdue repotting will generally dry out more quickly and benefits from being replanted into a larger pot. Topdressing pots with stones or moss can look attractive, but if you are finding watering difficult, avoid covering the soil until you get the hang of it.

How much light and warmth the plant gets, alongside how thirsty the plant is, will all affect how often it needs watering. This will vary as the seasons change, so be sure to keep a regular eye on it. Plants placed high up can be easy to forget about, so make checking on your plants part of a morning routine, or keep them somewhere easy to notice when they are getting thirsty. It's also better to water thoroughly, either by soaking the pot in a sink or watering through until water runs out of the bottom. This prevents parts of the soil from getting too dry and hydrophobic, meaning it will repel water rather than absorb it in the future.

Growing your plant in the correct compost mix will also help. Often plants are sold in less-than-ideal mixes, so repot at the earliest opportunity. Look out for (peat-free) houseplant mixes (including ones specifically for orchids and succulents), since these will be more free-draining than multi-purpose compost.

Houseplant feeds will support growth and flowers. You can either mix slow-release fertilizer into your compost when you repot the plant, or you can add feed to your watering can roughly every other time you water during the summer months. Make sure the plant is watered well when feeding to avoid scorching the roots with the chemicals in the feed. Liquid seaweed is a popular choice for a high nitrogen feed that can be found as organic and vegan-friendly. Certain plants, such as orchids, will have their own feeds available. For orchids, just use the feeds labelled 'bloom' rather than 'grow' throughout the year to help them flower more frequently.

Drop liquid houseplant feed into watering cans filled with water, following the instructions provided on the packaging to boost plant growth.

Pots and other kit

Enjoy using a watering can that is attractive and it won't matter if it gets left out on the side. Watering cans for houseplants are generally sold in 500ml–1 litre sizes (1–2 pints) and with long, thin spouts rather than with a rose head that you might use outdoors. The long spout allows you to get to the soil more easily and avoid getting water on the leaves or even worse, inside the base of the plant. Any moisture that sits inside it for long can lead to rot. Snips are a good idea for cutting back stems; use secateurs on anything thick or woody. While most people probably don't think about wearing gloves while handling plants, these are a good idea, especially if you have sensitive skin. The Horticultural Trades Association (HTA) has an online database of potentially harmful household plants (see p.134).

Misters come in all shapes and sizes and can double up as a handsome ornament. If you're growing plants inside a terrarium, there is a wide range of kit available. Browse tropical fish and aquarium shops for long scissors and tweezers, as well as tools made especially for terrariums. See the suppliers list at the end of the book for recommendations.

Pots can themselves be a joy, and it is possible to buy lovely and unusual handmade pieces that further add to the charm of growing plants. Compact plants such as cacti and succulents work the best for pots you want to be able to see well. When you buy a houseplant, make sure to keep it in the pot it comes in (known as the nursery pot), this will go inside a decorative cover pot. When it comes to potting up, you will need to replace both for a size up, but the old pots can be reused for smaller plants.

The nursery pot needs to have holes in the bottom and be slightly smaller than your decorative cover pot, so it isn't visible. A slightly oversized cover pot will also work fine but do use something to weigh it down inside to support and stabilize the nursery pot. For cover pots with holes, drip trays should be used underneath to prevent water damage.

When you repot, make sure roots are buried well (except for most orchids) but that the plant isn't any deeper in compost than it was before. Firm the plant in gently but well, as it is the contact between the roots and the soil that enables the roots to absorb water. Leave enough room between the compost and the top of the pot for watering. This is usually the depth of the nursery pot rim, which is intentionally the correct size for watering, relative to the size of each pot.

Whatever you are into, there is likely to be a pot designed to suit your taste and personal style.

Sustainability and safety

As with everything we do, it's best to operate as sustainably and environmentally friendly as possible. Houseplants connect us with nature, and this shouldn't come at a cost to the planet itself. Ensure you are buying peat-free when buying any type of compost.

It is also possible to minimize water waste when growing houseplants. Water by soaking multiple pots in the same water at the same time, or one after the other. If and when possible, use rainwater to water your plants – not only is it naturally high in nitrogen, which your plants will love, it will also reduce your mains water usage. As recommended earlier, seaweed fertilizer is available as organic, as well as a range of other natural feeds.

Avoiding single-use plastic is also becoming easier. Pots are now made in a range of materials and many retailers avoid selling plants in black plastic pots as these are harder to recycle, so you'll find them in taupe and other colours. It's always best to buy something that can be reused, and if not, is both recyclable and made of recycled material.

There is a huge amount of waste due to poor plant care and you can reduce this by looking after your plants. Keep your tender houseplants protected from outdoor elements; many are damaged and suffer shock once they leave shops and before they even reach our homes. Make sure that you buy houseplants that have been kept indoors, away from draughts and are healthy at point of sale.

While the online world makes it tantalizingly easier to find and buy a wide range of rare plants, doing a bit of homework will help you ensure that you aren't buying any that are being taken from the wild or protected by law. The International Union for Conservation of Nature (IUCN) has an online Red List of Threatened Species and you can check the name of any plant you are interested in before buying it. Do also check that any plant nurseries or garden centres you buy from operate as ethically and sustainably as you'd expect. Put your money where your passion is and support those businesses which are operating well; it's also great to support your local garden centres and shops. Once you are confident at growing houseplants, you may want to start propagating your own plants and swap or bulk up your own collection.

Do also consider keeping plants out of reach of pets or children if you have them and are unsure about the harmfulness through ingesting or touching them (see the Horticultural Trades Association (HTA) website on p.134 for more on toxicity).

When choosing houseplant potting mix, ensure any that you buy are peat-free.

Rooms

The joy of houseplants is that we're able to adorn our rooms with living objects, bringing life to walls and shelves, and softening hard edges and surfaces. We sometimes choose plants for spaces depending on how they make us feel; soft billowy foliage can create an oasis of calm and relaxation in bedrooms and bathrooms, while colourful foliage and blooms can add excitement and fun to areas for entertaining. We might have plants that remind us of family, friends or favourite holiday destinations, evoking happy memories. Houseplants might be chosen to complement other items on display or create cohesion in a room's design by repeating colours and patterns. We also might choose plants for certain scents that we enjoy. The perfumes can be pleasant or relaxing, a natural alternative to artificial fragrance or burning waxes that might add unwanted particles to the air. Some houseplants will even help purify the air in rooms through filtering out carbon dioxide and other unwanted chemicals. However, the number of plants required in each room to achieve any real impact in this sense is huge, so it is better instead to just appreciate that they can provide us with a more natural and healthier source of freshness to synthetic alternatives, such as sprays or candles.

While colour, texture and scent are great starting points, in order to keep a plant looking good, it's worth ensuring the conditions of the room suit the chosen plant. While all homes differ, the way in which we use them tends to be the same and the conditions similar due to location or use. Kitchens and bathrooms will have periods of higher humidity and temperature, while rooms upstairs are likely to be warmer and suffer less from draughts created by external doors as found downstairs. Hallways downstairs will often be darker and cooler, while any extension to the kitchen with skylights or a conservatory will usually be warmer and brighter.

In this section, we explore five different rooms and their typical settings to provide you with the guidelines for a better understanding of how to grow your plants in each area, as well as suggestions about which ones to use where. You'll find that within each room the light, temperature and humidity will also vary, as windows, radiators and furniture casting shade all create microclimates. We will look at five individual projects for each room, in order to explore the different conditions, as well as the opportunities and challenges of styling with houseplants that they all offer.

Hallway and stairs

The hallway is often the first room of a house that visitors encounter, and despite this great responsibility to welcome us home and make a wonderful first impression, it is one of the most challenging spaces in which to grow plants. Most hallways are not well-lit, nor are they particularly warm. The opening and closing of the front door also creates a huge change in temperature and humidity, especially during the colder months. While this doesn't mean we can't grow plants here, we do need to know which parts of the hallway are most suitable, and which plants will best tolerate these conditions.

The closer plants are to the front door, the more acutely they will experience a change in temperature as it opens and shuts, with the side of the hallway facing the door opening subjected to the most blasts of cold air in winter. Radiators must also be handled carefully, as while many have narrow shelves above them to help direct heat into the room, make sure you only choose plants to place here that are incredibly tough. The heat will dry out plants quickly, especially if placed in small pots for narrow shelves. The smaller a pot, the faster it will dry out, as it contains less moisture-holding compost. The hot air

around a radiator will also reduce humidity, so the plants in this area need to be watered more frequently. Often, we slow down watering in winter as plants absorb less with the reduced heat and light, but this is usually when radiators come on and can catch us off guard, resulting in plants suddenly drying out.

Hallways can also be tight on space and awkward to decorate; however, this does mean that when plants are used well, they can make the space more homely and pleasing. Use trailing plants on floating shelves in narrow spaces and those that can cope with lower light levels to grow in decorative pots on the floor. Walls near the stairs will benefit from light coming from above. Spaces opposite living rooms or kitchens will benefit from additional light too. If you do have windows, place plants around them; double glazed windows are a lot less likely to get cold or be draughty. Bigger pots present a lower risk of being knocked over with the passing of people and pets; keep any plant stands against a wall or in a corner to reduce the possibility of them toppling over. See the list on p.128 for suggestions of suitable plants to use in this area, in addition to those highlighted in the following projects.

Stairway gallery wall

Satin pothos (*Scindapsus pictus* 'Argyraeus')

With its speckled leaves, satin pothos is an attractive yet tough houseplant that will tolerate partial shade and is therefore useful in tricky rooms and spaces. This popular plant is a good choice to grow at height because the heart-shaped leaves trail down and can be best enjoyed at eye level. Its growth habit is also particularly voluptuous, growing up and out, as well as down. Grow on a wall space leading up a stairway if you have one and your hallway is particularly dim, as plants grown here are likely to benefit from additional light coming from upstairs.

To display these plants, keep them in their nursery pots and place securely inside attractive outer pots that can be attached to the wall. If the pots can sit flat against the wall, this will provide minimal obstruction to the stairway. Anything mounted at height needs to be done securely, so check the entire weight of the pots, plant and compost while wet, to ensure that attachment you use is strong enough to hold it all up. Outer pots can be permanently screwed into the wall or mounted in a way that they can be lifted up and off the wall, as required. Being able to care for the plants away from the stairs protects the area from mess.

A watering can with a long, narrow spout can be used to water the plants in place, if preferred, carefully and slowly. Be aware that plants at the top of the stairs are likely to dry out before those further down as they may receive more light and heat. To reduce the risk of moisture affecting the wall, remove the nursery pots and plunge them into a half-filled bucket, bathtub or sink of water, then leave to drain as required before replacing them in the outer pots. This also provides a more thorough watering as well as cleaning the leaves. Trim the trailing stems to suit your style, either neat and tidy, or looser for a more relaxed feel. The fewer leaves on each plant, the less often they will require watering, just take care not to remove more than a third of them at any one time for the health of the plant. See pp.118–119 for more information on satin pothos plant care.

Other small or trailing plants can also be grown and displayed in this way. In good light, plants such as the string of pearls (*Curio rowleyanus*) and other trailing succulents work well as they dry out slowly, and need less watering.

Space pots of satin pothos out evenly and parallel to the banister or stairs to create a pleasing display.

Brighten up a hallway

Peace lily (*Spathiphyllum wallisii*)

The shadier a spot is, the tougher it will be for any plant to thrive, but the peace lily is more tolerant than many other houseplants when it comes to lower levels of light. It actually prefers and will even grow better in some partial shade. As this plant is so popular, it's easy to get hold of a decent-sized specimen at a very reasonable price and pop it into a lovely decorative pot to use as a focal point in your hallway. While you should usually choose a decorative pot that is only about 2–3cm (approx. 1in) taller than the pot you bought the plant in, you can always prop the plant up inside a larger pot by placing large stones or other heavy material inside the decorative pot, before placing the plant pot inside. The stones will both anchor the display while giving the plant added height. You can also use pot feet to lift the pot slightly off the floor but do consider whether this is likely to cause marks on more delicate flooring. Ensure your plant pot is secure inside the outer pot, periodically checking for excess water and removing any dead leaves. A hammered metal pot will gently reflect and disperse any surrounding light, brightening up the area without creating any discernible reflections. Alternatively, any big,

bold and brightly coloured pot will similarly help lighten up a dark area.

Plants in cool, shady corners dry out more slowly, so check with your finger that the soil has mostly dried out before watering it, rather than just watering routinely. Peace lilies are very good at letting you know they're too dry before it's too late to remedy as the leaves will droop and sulk if the plant is not receiving enough, or too much water. Checking the moisture of the soil with your finger will let you know which of these it is. Add liquid plant feed to the water every other time you water throughout the summer to encourage buoyant growth and blooms. If the peace lily is still struggling to flower, swop it over every few weeks with a matching plant from a lighter part of the house, as this will boost flowers in the spring and autumn for both plants. Wipe the leaves with a damp cloth every few weeks to remove any dust and avoid getting tap water on the leaves to reduce unsightly water spots, created by salts and minerals in the water. Using five parts water and one part lemon juice or vinegar to wipe the leaves occasionally will help remove water spots (see pp.110–111 for more on peace lily care).

Peace lilies will tolerate some shade and are one of the easiest plants to keep looking good.

Front door décor

Ivy (*Hedera helix*)

If you have space inside your front door that you want to green up, you can do so with a tough and hardy plant such as ivy. Not always recognized for its houseplant potential as it grows so widely as a wild and garden plant, ivy will grow inside areas too cold and poorly lit for many other plants.

As a trailing and climbing plant, it's best grown in a pot on a stand or shelf. You may even choose to grow it spilling out of a large pot containing other plants. As an alternative to bringing some in from the garden, you can also buy it from plant nurseries or garden centres. Ivy is a particularly tough plant and can go straight from indoor to outside temperatures, but if you want to grow other plants somewhere cooler that have been grown in warmer conditions, harden them off first. Place a new plant somewhere near but which is not quite as cool as where you intend to display it permanently, for a couple of weeks, as this will prevent it suffering temperature shock.

Place one large plant or several smaller plants into a nursery pot half-filled with compost before adding more in. Firm in and ensure the root ball is covered by the compost. Multi-purpose compost mix, rather than more expensive houseplant mix, will work fine for ivy. Also, buying a bag of multi-purpose compost mix rather than reusing compost from the garden, will avoid bringing insects in from outside. Place this nursery pot inside a decorative cover pot of your choosing and place on a stand. If you are concerned about the stand being knocked over, consider discreetly attaching one of the back legs of the stand to the wall. This is also a consideration if the space is tight, the pot is small and light, or the stand is narrow and tall.

Keep the plant trim by using secateurs to snip at the growing stems or enjoy creating a more romantic look by letting it trail and grow. If the plant produces aerial roots from the stems to hold onto items, you can trim these off if not desired, or just let it grow wild. Do trim back any stems that get too close to the wall to avoid aerial roots sticking and potentially creating damage to paint or wallpaper. Canes, a slender moss pole or trellis can also be pushed into the pot enabling the plant to climb. Ivy will cope with some forgotten watering, but do water when dry, and keep a close eye while the roots establish. Find more on growing ivy on pp.100–101.

Ivy makes for a surprising indoor plant, but will cope with low light and cold areas better than most other plants.

Adorn a radiator cover

Cast iron plant (*Aspidistra elatior*)

Growing plants above a radiator is not for the faint-hearted, but neither is it impossible. Ensure the radiator is kept to a lower setting and choose tough plants to grow there, particularly those that can handle both strong heat and drying out. In a sunny spot, cacti and succulents are an obvious choice as they cope better with heat and the low humidity created by the radiator. However, in a hallway, you may need to find a plant that can also manage low levels of light and cold temperatures when the heating is off, or the door left open. The cast iron plant (*Aspidistra elatior*) is so-called because of having what often gets described as an iron constitution; it's also known as 'bullet proof', probably the toughest of all the houseplants and a great choice.

Choose a pot size according to your plant and space. Remember the bigger the pot, the more compost it will contain and therefore the longer it will take to dry out. If you can only fit a small pot in the space, check on it frequently and keep your choice of plant small. Removing a few leaves will reduce the speed at which the plants will transpire and lose moisture, just do this in moderation and never more than a third at once. From autumn through to spring and summer, the plant will not require much care at all, and is tolerant of a few forgotten waterings. However, once the radiator comes on in winter do keep an eye on the plant and the soil. Trim off any yellowing leaves; you can even trim off any brown tips using a pair of snips or scissors.

Clean leaves with a damp cloth and mist to help temporarily raise the humidity immediately around the plant. Fortunately, as the plant is a slow grower, it won't need repotting often and won't quickly outgrow the space. If the plant does get too big, you can divide it by breaking up the root ball and repotting half of it. Always look for parts of the plant that are younger and healthier to use if you don't want to keep all the plant material.

Keep the plant in a nursery pot with holes in, inside a decorative cover pot – this will make it easier to water. Remove and soak the whole pot in water before letting it drain out and returning it to its place. For a particularly narrow shelf space, consider potting the plant into a long rectangular pot or container to maximise the space available and provide more compost inside the pot. Find more on growing a cast iron plant on pp.92–93.

Possibly the hardest plant to kill, the cast iron plant is the best choice for a spot that most other plants can't tolerate.

Living room

Living rooms tend to have bigger windows than other parts of the house and therefore more natural light. These rooms for entertaining are also where we get to relax and be ourselves, and therefore are well worth adorning with plants. Not only do they usually contain larger areas of indirect bright light, but are also often kept warm, and have a generally stable relative humidity – all great growing conditions for most houseplants.

The area a couple of metres around, but not right up to, the biggest window will get the most useful light. The further from the window and the higher up you are, the less light you will get. Watch out for dark spaces above tall furniture, behind chimney breasts, bookcases or behind sofa arms, as these may be quite shady. However, these spaces do lend themselves as homes for plants that are sensitive to too much light and prefer semi-shade. Again, watch out for radiators that will dry out plants; this also includes in front of and close to, as well as on top.

If your window receives direct sunlight, the windowsill or bay should be restricted to the use of plants that cope well with bright light and are at less at risk of scorch. Cacti, succulents and many plants native to South Africa or desert regions will thrive here. This is not a space for plants from jungle floors with dappled light. Also, be aware that if your window is not double glazed it may also get quite draughty; you'll know if it is letting in cold air as on cooler days you should be able to feel a cool breeze around it. Growing here will be fine in the warmer months, but may cause problems for tender plants as the temperature drops outside in winter.

With good light and other growing conditions, the living room is the place to enjoy presenting some wow-factor plants. These could be large, colourful plants or those with interesting flowers and foliage that create a focal point in the room. These may also be your investment plants, ones that you buy as more expensive mature specimens, or are particularly flamboyant. Consider the colour already in your living room, especially on the walls and furniture. In garden design, try to limit your use of hard materials to just three different types, minimizing clashes and creating too much visual noise. Do this indoors by matching the colour or type of material such as wood, tile or stone with your pot choice if you already have three distinct colours, patterns or textures in the room.

Bay window beauty

Bird of paradise (*Strelitzia reginae*)

Any space directly in front of a window is a wonderful space for the right plants. These are the ones that enjoy bright light (also referred to as full sun) and are usually from hot regions, as you might expect. Many of these sun-loving plants grow well enough in indirect bright light, but never as well as they could, and this includes the process of producing buds and flowering successfully. The bird of paradise flower is one example. It is often used as a houseplant just for foliage as without enough hours of bright light, typically 4–6 hours a day, it won't bloom. While the large leaves are attractive, the flowers are remarkable and will turn heads in your home. See p.82–83 for more guidance.

As the bird of paradise plant can grow up to 2m (6½ft) tall, a large space such as a bay window can provide a stage on which to show off its magnificent flowers. With larger plants, using heavier and larger pots will help keep them stable, and reduce the risk of them being knocked over. If you don't have a space like this, but somewhere else warm and sunny, ideally on the slightly humid side, you can also grow this plant there.

Another design rule, used both in home and garden, is the sacred beauty of the odd number. When you can, group your plants in threes and fives or as a solo performer. Generally thought to create more interest and be more effective at capturing the gaze, it's possible that objects grouped in odd numbers just appears more natural and less staged. Even numbers can create beautiful symmetry, but what is not symmetrical about the display sticks out like a sore thumb, and it can all look overly arranged and static.

While you may choose to grow just one bird of paradise or similar *objet d'art* plant, the benefit of growing multiple plants is that you are more likely to have flowers at any given time. With the right conditions, specifically enough light, it is possible for them to flower at any point in the year. A group of plants also creates a more impressive display. Arrange your large pots so that they overlap slightly, with your tallest plant in the middle; this will create a pleasing pyramid effect, drawing the eye up to the blooms. For a plant that looks as classically beautiful as a bird of paradise, consider the use of a simple but luxurious terracotta pot to set it off and not compete with the exotic colours of the blooms.

Embrace direct light by growing one or more head-turning bird of paradise plants in a space where many other plants may be scorched.

Coffee table terrarium

Bun moss (*Leucobryum glaucum*), pink mosaic plant (*Fittonia albivenis* 'Pink Angel') and parlour palm (*Chamaedorea elegans*)

If you have a room with good light but is too draughty for the plants you'd like to grow, a solution is to place them inside a closed terrarium. Perhaps your front door opens straight onto your living room, or your windows are full of character but not double-glazed. Plants inside a closed terrarium are also less likely to dry out if you forget to water them or go away on holiday. In terrariums, very little moisture can escape, so they keep themselves hydrated.

The temperature inside a closed glass terrarium will also be a bit warmer than the air outside it. The display acts like a miniature greenhouse, which is beneficial to all plants that enjoy humid, warm conditions more typically found in a bathroom or kitchen, although it is worth noting that any succulent plants will quickly rot in this sort of environment. However, should you like the aesthetic of a terrarium and want to grow cacti or other succulents inside one, look out for open terrariums. These do require watering, but can make great displays for miniature desert scenes and offer some protection if the plants have spines.

Don't place a terrarium on a windowsill as you will be multiplying the effects of the glass and end up with very hot conditions. A terrarium where more than a third of the glass has fogged up indicates that the conditions are too hot and/or wet. If this is the case, open it up to wipe the glass dry and move it somewhere a little less sunny. Generally, a space 1m (3¼ft) or so away from a window is ideal. In a living room this may mean in the middle of the floor, which is why a coffee table can be make for a useful stand for your terrarium.

Books and websites offer a whole range of advice, but the combination of bun moss to cover the soil, a pretty foliage plant like the pink mosaic plant and a structural plant like a very young parlour palm work well and are easy to source. These plants all also enjoy the same light conditions, which ranges from semi-shade to indirect bright light. Always select plants that enjoy the same conditions and require similar watering to make caring for them easier and ultimately successful. For more information on growing mosaic plants and parlour plants see pp.104–105 and 108–109 respectively.

A terrarium on a coffee table can be enjoyed from all sides and will entertain guests.

Grow lights, a bright idea

Heart-leaf philodendron (*Philodendron scandens*)

Any room in the home may have corners that are naturally too dark to successfully grow plants in. Thanks to LED grow lights, this issue can now be easily resolved, displaying healthy and beautiful plants in a wider range of locations – including the living room where plants may be most enjoyed by visitors. Lights designed specifically to support plant growth have recently come a long way in design. Some are now almost indistinguishable from domestic light bulbs. Many LED bulbs are now available that can provide all wavelengths of light but displaying just a warm, white glow. When purchasing a grow light, do first just check that the one you buy provides a full spectrum of light and that you are able to source an adaptor to fit the bulb into your light stand or desired light fitting if required; many but not all screw straight into standard fixtures. Artificial lights must always be fitted above plants to produce upward growth and the optimal distance of the light from the plant will depend on the strength and brand of the bulb. Generally, they need to be placed relatively close to the plant: for best results read and follow the manufacturers' instructions.

Grow lights can also be used to supplement the natural light that is available during the shorter days of the winter months. Place grow lights above plants that require the most light and use timers so that they come on just before sunset. This will provide a few additional hours of light, and other plants nearby will also benefit from this extra boost. Do make sure the lights are only on for a few hours and not all night, as not only is this an unnecessary cost, but plants also require day and night cycles in order to remain healthy, rest and grow.

Make a feature of a dark corner in your living room by installing a hanging houseplant with a light over it. Screw an LED grow light bulb into a light fitting with a plant in a pot attached underneath. This will add both charm and additional ambient lighting to your room. One plant that will grow happily in a lit hanging basket or pot is heart-leaf philodendron. It's easy to grow and glossy, heart-shaped leaves will trail out of a hanging pot, as the name suggests. Place the plant pot inside a decorative outer pot so that it can be removed and soaked in water, then allowed to drain out before being put back in. See pp.98–99 for more on caring for this plant.

Plants such as the heart-leaf philodendron work well as hanging plants and will enjoy extra light in a dim corner.

Dressing up a bookcase

String of hearts (*Ceropegia woodii*)

Whether you arrange your books by colour, size or have them all facing the other way around, you are likely to have some space on each shelf to adorn with plants. Place compact plants like stout cacti, or trailing plants like string of hearts, in the gaps between books, in front of them or whichever way looks right. A bookcase opposite a window is a good candidate for dressing with plants as it will benefit from facing the light. However, do remember that each shelf will receive a different amount of sunshine. The shelves high up and low down will likely receive the least amount of light if your window is set from the middle of the wall upwards. On a tall bookcase, the shelves around chest height are likely to receive the most light. Placing plants above your eyeline relies on a good memory for checking whether they need watering, so is best avoided unless you are vigilant.

Your mixture of books and plants can be made even more appealing by selecting a range of complementary, creative and unusual pots to place the plants in. Faces, animals, torsos and unusual objects will all create the feel of a 'cabinet of curiosities'. Look out for handmade pots in natural or eclectic shapes and colours, or make your own. Kits are available that allow you to easily create small clay pots without the need of a kiln and may appeal to those with a more artistic streak.

The string of hearts plant will cascade over a shelf or two, its ornate and charming leaves appearing almost unreal. It will work well with a spiky cactus, the cactus providing texture and contrast to the draping stems and variegated foliage. Also, as both are succulents, they are likely to require a similar amount of occasional watering. Either remove the plants in order to water them or water carefully and slowly on the shelf to avoid damage. String of hearts and other trailing plants can be arranged as you feel works best; you may find that small, clear plastic clips with adhesive on the back will allow you to train any trailing plant as you wish along a shelf and down the side of the bookcase.

Both trailing plants and cacti work well grown on a higher shelf. This allows them the space to grow as well the safety from being knocked over. Plants with spines are also kept out of harm's way. With adequate light, string of hearts will produce pretty little flowers. See pp.122–123 for more information.

The string of hearts plant can be styled alongside other contrasting plants to add interesting detail to a bookcase.

Kitchen and kitchen extensions

The kitchen can be a fantastic place for plants to grow, especially if yours has an extension, a skylight, generous-sized windows or a glass door to the outside. A bit like a super-charged living room, not only will you typically find good light for at least some of the day, but also a warm temperature and above-average humidity. The heat and moisture will come from the oven, dishwasher or washing machine. If your kitchen is on the small and darker side, make the most of the window space, placing pots on the windowsill and hang plants from the ceiling using hanging planters or macramé. Choose plants that tolerate semi-shade or low light for areas that are blocked from the light coming in through windows.

Plants related to food have an obvious appeal; these can create delicious scents as well as be useful for cooking. Pots of herbs can be grown on windowsills and fruit trees on counters that receive ample light. Be aware that guests may not find the presence of soil in close proximity to their food appetizing, which is why a barrier such as a kitchen sink, growing up on shelves with cookbooks or in a large pot on a counter where the compost is

not visible may be a smart choice. Keep your plants wiped clean of dust and remove any water sitting in the bottom of pots to keep both your plants and other people happy.

There can be too much of a good thing: watch out for plants placed too close to large windows or under skylights. Ensure you are placing plants that tolerate bright light in these positions and move them a few inches out of direct light to avoid scorching in the height of summer. Areas around kettles, stove tops and the oven will produce high heat as well as steam: you'll soon notice damage to leaves if a plant is too close to anything hot.

As with any other room, you can decorate with as many or as few plants as suits your taste and style. Hanging planters come in a wide range of designs from fabrics to metals, so there is plenty of choice to find something to suit your kitchen. Do check that plants don't get in the way of units with doors; trailing plants above a fridge or cabinet will become bothersome every time you need to open it. However, a few key plants can be used in empty spaces, including the floor, to create a welcoming and pleasant environment.

Orange tree on a tabletop

Calamondin orange (*Citrus × macrocarpa*)

Brighten up your kitchen with a touch of the Mediterranean by growing a miniature orange tree. The calamondin orange is the best-suited for a houseplant as it's easy to grow and can provide attractive flowers all year round as well as fruit in summer. A breakfast counter or kitchen island makes a great spot to enjoy the tree from all sides, plus it perks up mornings with its fresh, sweet citrus scent – a nice companion to the smell of tea or coffee. If your kitchen space is smaller or not so well-lit, choose a spot on a sunny windowsill. The calamondin orange is slow-growing so won't quickly outgrow its space and you can prune it to keep the shape compact.

Choose a nice decorative cover pot – a glossy blue in combination with the yellow or orange fruit is suggestive of the South of France, Spain or Morocco, as is the use of terracotta. A rectangular pot will contrast with the pendant fruit, providing a variety of shape, or you can mirror the roundness of the top of the plant with a matching circular pot. If the inside of the pot is visible and unappealing, top-dress with moss or gravel to cover it up, but do remember to check underneath for watering. Curling leaves will be a sure sign that the plant is thirsty; reaching this point will risk developing flower buds falling off.

If your kitchen is spacious, you can place multiple orange trees around the room against the walls, on the floor or on stands, creating the feel of a historic orangery. Orangeries were first built in the 17th century to house these exotic plants where winter climates would not allow.

You might want to consider extending your citrus collection with lemon and lime trees, which will complement an orange tree, or other scented plants. However, do be aware that growing several perfumed houseplants in one room can create an overwhelming combination of aromas. Choose subtle and similar scents, avoiding any contrasting or clashing fragrances. Unlike plants grown outdoors, scents will hang around and build up, especially in smaller, bright and warm spaces.

Should you feel particularly enthused about growing oranges, full-sized trees are available, but a calamondin orange grown on a counter, windowsill or stand will provide fruit and flowers at a fraction of the cost, and at the right height can be enjoyed at eye level. See pp.90–91 for more on growing this plant.

The calamondin orange is the easiest citrus to grow as a small houseplant and it produces a lovely scent.

Succulent windowsill display

Combination of succulents

While any sunny windowsill is a great space to grow cacti and other succulents, a kitchen window provides a spot out of reach for both the protection of people and the plants themselves. If your kitchen looks out onto a garden or outdoor space, it's also likely to receive good, unobstructed sunlight. Windowsills are sometimes quite narrow, another reason why slow-growing cacti and other succulents are a good choice; it will be a long time before they need a bigger space.

Do make sure you don't buy plants with artificial flowers added – this also happens with bird of paradise flowers – so be aware. The cacti selected here are ones that are easier to care for and bloom more than many others. The suggested plants, left to right, are: bunny ears cactus (*Opuntia* spp.), German cactus (*Cochemiea guelzowiana* also known as *Mammillaria guelzowiana*), lace aloe (*Aristaloe aristata* 'Green Pearl'), rebutia (*Aylostera deminuta*) and the moonstone plant (*Pachyphytum oviferum*). These have all been chosen for a combination of shape, texture, blooms and ease of growing, but do opt for whichever cacti and succulents take your fancy – they will all enjoy this space.

The German cactus is actually from Mexico and produces pink flowers in late spring/summer. The rebutia also produces lovely flowers and the bunny ears cactus is popular for its shape. All three can be cared for in the same way. The lace aloe and moonstone plant will provide you with wonderful contrasting shapes and can be grown in the same way as other succulents such as Mexican snowball (*Echeveria elegans*) (see pp.102–103).

The space above a sink, or windowsill elsewhere in the kitchen is likely to be symmetrical and uniform. This presents you with the wonderful opportunity to be creative with both your pots and plants. Nothing needs to match – your display can be a performance of colour, shape and texture, so go with it and enjoy combining different plants. Alternating the cacti with smoother succulents will create rhythm, and a display made using odd numbers will always look more attractive. By keeping the tallest to the side, it will be easier to care for the others. If you are right-handed it can be helpful to keep the biggest and most spiny plants to the far left for ease of watering as you move along; left-handers should do the reverse.

Plants shown left to right on a kitchen windowsill: bunny ears cactus (*Opuntia* spp.), German cactus (*Cochemiea guelzowiana*), lace aloe (*Aristaloe aristata* 'Green Pearl'), rebutia (*Aylostera deminuta*) and the moonstone plant (*Pachyphytum oviferum*).

Green up a kitchen corner

Peacock plant (*Goeppertia orbifolia*)

Having explored two very sunny positions in a lovely warm and slightly humid kitchen, it's worth addressing the slightly shady corners that are also likely to exist, and how to best use these to your advantage. There are many beautiful foliage plants that can be bought from large home furnishing stores as well as garden centres at a reasonable price. One of the most handsome, and easiest to grow, is the peacock plant (*Goeppertia orbifolia* also known as *Calathea orbifolia*).

This plant will enjoy the slight humidity of the kitchen. Any houseplant with large, thin leaves is more susceptible to becoming brown and crispy at the edges in drier rooms, meaning the kitchen can be a great spot to grow one in. A corner provides space for a medium-sized plant or one that can get quite large as it is out of the way and less likely to be knocked over. Alocasias, philodendrons and Swiss cheese plants will also work well in a kitchen, as long as there is some light.

While the peacock plant enjoys indirect bright light, it will also tolerate a bit of shade, which makes it ideal for placing behind kitchen counters or to the side of a window. If your kitchen window is not particularly bright, areas nearby (rather than in front) will likely not receive much daylight. Any bright light will damage the dramatic leaves, so do find a spot out of direct sun. The plant will be happy in most parts of your kitchen as well as other rooms. See pp.112–113 for more information.

Pick a lovely big cover pot and keep it either on the floor or higher up on a spare chair or stand. When choosing where to place your plant, watch out for the position of radiators, draughty windows or external doors; it will be happier away from any extremes of temperature or gusty air. Looked after and in the right space, the peacock plant will always look bright and fresh, perfect for a kitchen with a clean feel. It is perky, fast-growing, and will regularly put out young new leaves to replace the fading, older ones. Remove any damaged leaves to encourage new growth and keep it looking good.

Dust the leaves and wipe with a damp cloth as needed; plants in the kitchen should be kept cleaner than anywhere else for hygiene reasons. Making sure your plants are dust-free will also keep the decorative round leaves glossy, healthy and better able to photosynthesize.

The peacock plant will happily tolerate a slightly shady part of the kitchen and most other rooms with slightly lower light levels.

Spotlight on a focal point plant

Fiddle-leaf fig (*Ficus lyrata*)

Not all corners are dark, and if your kitchen benefits from an airy extension or is itself big and light, you'll have spaces that are perfect for more architectural statement plants. The fiddle-leaf fig (*Ficus lyrata*) is a great space filler, and while it can be tricky to grow in shady rooms with low humidity, a well-lit corner in a kitchen or kitchen extension is the perfect spot. The plant grows in full sun naturally, so will thrive in conditions too harsh for other foliage plants with thinner and more delicate leaves. It's a popular and fashionable tree as a houseplant, adored by interior designers, and for this reason has become more widely available and therefore more affordable.

The brighter the light in the room, the faster the plant is more likely to use up the water it absorbs. Check on the plant every few days and water roughly every week in the summer, and then less so during the darker months. Ethically made decorative cover pots of natural materials such as woven seagrass or water hyacinth can lend a soft touch to living rooms, conservatories and kitchen extensions. Alternatively large white pots, or ones chosen to complement the colour scheme in your room work well, but do make sure the plant is not top-heavy, especially if using fabric cover pots. The fiddle-leaf fig can grow quickly, so either trim back top growth to your desired shape, or add weights to the decorative pot. Placing other medium-sized plants in pots in front will also help to anchor it. The corner of a room is a good spot for plants that are large, providing support from behind if needed, as well as preventing them from getting in the way. For more information on growing and caring for a fiddle-leaf fig, see pp.96–97.

Fiddle-leaf figs are also used to decorate well-lit bedrooms, but if you have more light and space downstairs (including good ceiling height) this will be a better spot for the plant. Grown in an entertaining space, it can also be enjoyed by your guests and used to enhance the feel of the area. If your living spaces are a neutral colour, the soft green leaves gently add depth to the room. The real magic is in the leaves, as their texture is different on each side. The tops of the leaves are glossy, so they'll subtly bounce light around the room, while the undersides are matte, making them easy on the eyes as they diffuse the light they reflect and provide a lovely, textural contrast.

Where there is plenty of space and light, make the most of it with a fiddle-leaf fig.

Bedroom

Houseplants transform rooms into cosy, secluded spaces, and nowhere is this more beneficial than in the bedroom. Here, plants connect us to nature and provide patterns that help settle the mind, both wonderfully conducive to sleep. We know that treating our senses to calming scents and gentle colours makes us feel more serene, so implement this at home with the use of some select plants.

Look for plants with big foliage that have a soft texture or decorative flowers, or with scents that you find relaxing. Even plants that you might grow in the garden can often be grown indoors, just make sure Mediterranean plants such as lavender have access to bright light, are grown in free-draining compost mix and aren't overwatered. I love the scent of real jasmine (*Jasminum officinale*), but if you find it too tricky to care for, grow Madagascar jasmine (*Stephanotis floribunda*) instead. It's easier to grow and its white flowers produce a similar scent. Many plants that bloom are often sold in small pots that dry out quickly. Make your life easier by potting them up as soon as is convenient, but do wait until your plant has finished flowering, as disturbing it will likely hasten the end of its blooms.

There are plants that wind and trail, creating a whimsical feel. I don't particularly enjoy sleeping with anything on the wall above my head, but for the more courageous, plants can be trained across this area using clear adhesive wall hooks. Alternatively, train stems of climbers such as pothos around the area next to the bed and up other furniture. As your bedroom is likely to be a private space, you can be more creative with your houseplant décor. Use a small hammock on the wall to hold a plant, hang a string of hearts like a chandelier or combine a mixture of plants and art prints on the wall. There is great freedom in the intimacy of the bedroom space.

The growing conditions of bedrooms will vary, but hopefully you'll have a spot that suits a wide range of plants. Perhaps you benefit from the additional humidity of an ensuite bathroom or the added warmth of a hot water tank nearby. Your bedroom might have the lowest light level of all your rooms, but just pick your plants accordingly. If it's dimly lit, refer back to the chapter on hallways. Look around the space and work out where you get the best light, and which are your shady corners. If you don't use the room much, such as with spare bedrooms, opt for plants that are lower maintenance, such as the parlour palm (*Chamaedorea elegans*) to make life easier when it comes to watering.

Fancy up a bedroom

Parlour palm (*Chamaedorea elegans*)

The parlour palm was famously used in living rooms (or rather parlours) by the Victorians who were very taken with it. However, with so many more options at our disposal than the Victorians, you can choose more exciting plants to decorate there and save the palm for a bedroom. One of the benefits of the parlour palm is that it so easy to care for and will cope with a little bit of neglect, making it a perfect candidate for a corner that might get missed sometimes or gets less light. As it's widely available in large home furnishing stores as well as garden centres, it's also very affordable to buy at a mature size for instant impact. The shape of the finely cut leaves creates a lovely calming effect, leaves overlapping each other and gently curving in shape (see pp.108–109 for more on the parlour palm).

A tall, upright plant is ideal for a corner, especially next to a door as it is less likely to get in the way. Ornamental objects such as lamps and sculptures can also be placed around or next to it, creating a charming display as well as making the most of the space on the floor. Any plant directly on the floor deserves a lovely big pot, something that enhances its status as a statement and focal point. Decorative pots with a brushed metal finish look smart but informal. Alternatively, ceramic pots, matte or glazed, or wicker, bamboo and other woven materials offer a soft range of options to complement the fabrics of your bed throw, cushions, carpet or rugs. Make sure that the plant is kept inside a nursery pot with drainage holes before being placed inside a cover pot, and that the cover pot itself is waterproof.

For a similar plant with quirkier leaves, opt for the kentia palm (*Howea fosteriana*). Its leaves are brighter green than those of the parlour palm, shorter and wider, but still in wispy fans. Its maintenance needs are similar, but just a tad less forgiving than the parlour palm.

If a room corner does get good light, you can also consider a plant with twisted stems such as an Indian laurel (*Ficus microcarpa*) or the lovely money tree (*Pachira aquatica*) for sculptural interest. The money tree is a popular houseplant that is easy to grow with good light, but likes to not dry out. This may be a problem if you are forgetful about watering, but great if you tend to overwater; just make sure it doesn't end up sitting in a pool of water.

Create a relaxing environment with the attractive foliage of the low maintenance parlour palm.

Plants for small spaces

Black velvet elephant ear (*Alocasia* 'Black Velvet')

Small decorative plants can be placed on desks or bedside tables, where they won't get lost and can be best viewed. Buying smaller plants can make them cheaper, as in many cases they don't take as long to grow to a suitable size.

There are those who believe in various 80:20-type rules when it comes to household clutter. One school of thought suggests that only 20 per cent of your belongings should be on show inside your home to prevent untidiness. If you have just a couple of items kept out on a desk, a small plant is one that will enhance the surroundings and lift the room's aesthetic. Black velvet elephant ear is a lovely dwarf houseplant that is less common and will offer visual interest. The plant stays small and grows slowly, but most importantly has quietly stunning foliage. Pale veins strike through dark, velvety green leaves; the plant appears almost to be made of an exquisite and luxurious fabric.

You mustn't let *Alocasia* 'Black Velvet' dry out, but if you do use your desk regularly, it's a good space to keep an eye on a special houseplant. It will also require indirect bright light, so ensure your desk isn't in front of a window or facing one if you get lots of strong light, while still making sure it does get some soft sunshine. *Alocasia* 'Black Velvet' also needs good drainage, so check the pot inside the cover pot has holes in it. The plant prefers a slightly higher-than-average room humidity, so keep it out of the way of any draughts (see pp.84–85 for more information). For lower light levels, consider other plants with interesting foliage, such as *Syngonium* 'Pixie', which has variegated, arrow-shaped leaves, and is less expensive, but like black velvet elephant ear also needs to be checked regularly for watering.

The bedside table should be reserved for objects that make you happy, and perhaps evoke special memories. While you may keep items that are functional, you might also consider adding a miniature rose or other plant you'll enjoy admiring each morning. Other than compact plants, trailing plants like the creeping fig (*Ficus pumila*) can tumble down the side of a table with delicate leaves or, if you are likely to forget to water plants here, consider architectural succulents, providing that the room has good light. I would avoid placing cacti near the bed, but a softer choice such as *Echeveria* 'Blue Bird' can look attractive in a small, elegant pot.

Place plants that require more attention (such as the black velvet elephant ear) somewhere you will see them regularly up close.

Ornamental windowsills

False shamrock (*Oxalis triangularis*)

A bright windowsill can be a mixed blessing. It may be the perfect home for desert plants such as cacti and other succulents, but it is also somewhere many other plants will become scorched, making it a tricky spot.

The false shamrock is a plant that looks far too beautiful and delicate considering how robust it really is, and it will grow well on a bright windowsill. This plant is suited for a room in which you might enjoy the sunrise or sunset as its leaves move like butterfly wings, but very slowly, during those parts of the day. They close at night and then open up again in the morning. It's very low maintenance and is able to recover quickly from drying out. The tough plant grows from corms, which are bulb-like structures, meaning that even when all the foliage and stems have died back from thirst after weeks of neglect, a good soak will usually recover the plant and produce new growth. The false shamrock plant has beautiful markings on its dark purple leaves, delicate flowers and it's easy to pull off any dead material. For more information on growing this plant, see pp.94–95.

With bright light and usually a place in the eyeline from anywhere in the room, a windowsill is a wonderful place to showcase a plant that will cope with full sun. For a plant with more variety in options available, you could also grow a pelargonium. This plant will produce beautiful flowers and even scented leaves if you choose one such as *Pelargonium* 'Lemon Fizz' or 'Prince of Orange'. These plants will grow well in full sun, and can better tolerate drier soil, but won't cope and recover as well as a false shamrock, so do stick with that if it is likely to be neglected. Opting for a pelargonium opens up a whole world of choice, and in an area that you want to display an elegant and sophisticated plant, perhaps choose an interesting species rather than a cultivar. A 'species' is a plant that has not been bred for ornamental use, and is as you would find it in the wild. *Pelargonium sidoides* is a bit of a plant geek's choice: it's a wild plant rather than a cultivar, less often seen in homes and produces delicate, dark purple flowers and greyish foliage. Alternatively, an easier selection that will put on a show of plentiful foliage and vigorous flowers is *Pelargonium* 'Best Red' and other popular cultivars. For more information on growing pelargoniums, see pp.114–115.

The false shamrock is surprisingly low maintenance for a plant with delicate blooms and unusual foliage.

Statement plant on a stand

Swiss cheese plant (*Monstera deliciosa*)

Plant stands are invaluable for displaying houseplants. Not only are you able to position a plant to its best advantage, but you can increase the amount of light it gets and make a medium-sized plant appear much bigger. There is a range of stands available to suit every taste and budget. Antique designs are a sustainable choice that can add character to a scheme, for example simple Arts and Crafts stands work well in a variety of modern interiors. In many styles of bedrooms, contemporary step ladder style stands are popular as they have an informal feel and provide at least two levels to accommodate several plants. They allow plants to trail if placed on the lower steps, leaving a space for a plant needing height above it.

Foldable stands are great for small spaces, as they can be stored away as required. If your plant and its compost mix are not particularly heavy, choose a heavy cover pot with a wide base, and make sure you place the stand against a wall for extra support.

Once you've got a stand to maximize the space in your bedroom, you have the opportunity to choose a statement plant that will be your main feature and create a focal point. If your room is well-lit, but out of direct light, you have a wide range of options to choose from. Plants with particularly large, shapely leaves such as the Swiss cheese plant are a popular choice for good reason. Beloved by mid-20th century architects, the distinctive, perforated leaves of this plant have become iconic of the houseplant trend. As the light shines into your bedroom, you'll also be able to enjoy the wonderful silhouette created on the wall from the plant's shadow. It's a climbing plant, so will require more support, such as a moss-covered pole stuck into the pot if you intend to let it grow to a large size. With favourable conditions it's possible to grow to over 4m (13ft), turning a bedroom into a jungle-like oasis. This plant requires watering every couple of weeks (see pp.124–125).

If your room does not get enough light for a Swiss cheese or similar foliage plant, there are other medium-sized statement plants that will tolerate lower light levels, such as the ZZ plant (*Zamioculcas zamiifolia*). This plant is particularly easy to care for and has a brilliant, bold structure. The rigid leaves are produced on diagonal growth and the plant will sit proudly on a stand.

Place a Swiss cheese plant on a stand for added height and impact.

Bathroom

Not only are bathrooms a great environment for houseplants that love humidity to thrive, but the rooms themselves also benefit from having plants in them. A bland and sterile area can be transformed into an indulgent or holistic, spa-like space with stylish and creative use of greenery.

Since most bathrooms don't have blinds or curtains, they often have plenty of light, even more so if windows are facing the direction that provides the most sun. Frosted windows are even better for houseplants. The ample sunlight coming through is diffused, creating that bright indirect light that provides plenty of light without the scorch of direct sun.

Plants from tropical jungles or anywhere else naturally humid will especially enjoy the additional humidity during and after a shower or bath. This will help prevent plants with papery leaves curl up and dry out. Avoid placing plants in any areas that might be exposed to extreme temperatures, such as by windows that might be swung open unexpectedly by gusts or radiators that get very hot. More sensitive plants won't tolerate the shock of a big change in temperature.

Choose the right plants for a bathroom and they will be easy to grow, as the favourable conditions are doing half the job for you. Be aware this is obviously not the space to grow desert plants or succulents that will need periods of drying out if the room frequently becomes very humid and wet, but most other plants will live happily in a well-lit bathroom setting. If your bathroom is a good size, you may still get shady corners, so choose plants to place there that will tolerate lower light levels. Also, if the room is small, hanging plants are a great way to save space. The plants you choose can easily be used to match the style of your bathroom.

Plants can be added to windowsills to increase privacy if the glass isn't frosted, and anywhere from bath racks to floor space provides a wide range of spaces to display different plants with varying growth habits. Plants will take longer to dry in a humid environment, which means less watering for you, and as long as your plants are humidity-loving, they are less likely to suffer from rot. However, make sure you still water around the base of plants and don't leave water sitting in the bottom of the pot to reduce the risk of roots rotting. Also, remove dead or dying plant material to maintain plant health and hygiene.

Air plants by a window

Combination of air plants

Air plants are popular as they are easy to care for, as well as looking wonderfully unusual. Their foliage is incredibly shapely, and they can produce flowers in exotic hues of pinks and blues. They are quite otherworldly; some almost resemble sea creatures and offer a suitably coastal feel to a bathroom. There is a wide range of air plants available, from Spanish moss (*Tillandsia usneoides*) to the ornamental *T. stricta* and *T. xerographica*. It's worth exploring online and in specialist shops as there is a wider range than initially meets the eye, with a broad array of foliage and exotic blooms.

Some growers enjoy using glue to attach air plants to pieces of driftwood and decorative shells; there are even design kits available should you want to get crafty. However, you may find that a simple approach is best, using a couple of extra materials to enhance the display of an air plant to show it off.

It's possible to buy an air plant alone or accompanied by supporting material in which to display it. Hanging air terrariums are popular; these are glass bulbs that hang from above with large openings. These protect the plant from draughts and keep the immediate area around the plant slightly more humid, while still allowing much-needed air flow. This is useful if you want to grow air plants in a room other than a bathroom with some protection. Stones used as weights with wire twisted around them are also used as holders. These allow you to choose which way up you want to display your plant, meaning you can play with the shape of the plant. However attractive it is, make sure you avoid using anything with copper wire directly touching plant material as high levels of it is toxic to plants, especially when repeatedly wet, as the reactivity of the copper is increased. Growing in soil will also harm air plants as they'll rot, so don't be tempted to grow in or on soil mixes.

White macramé hangers can also look very effective, especially with *T. xerographica*, which grows in a clump with broad foliage twisting away from the centre. Ensure that wherever you choose to display your air plants they get a few hours of indirect bright light and are easy to remove from their support to soak in water. You can mist air plants but soaking them all together in tepid water as required will provide better hydration and encourage better flowering. For more on growing air plants, see pp.78–79.

Hang roundish air plants such as *Tillandsia xerographica* in macramé to show off their shape and *T. stricta* on stands to allow blooms to be seen at their best.

Ferns for the floor

Boston fern (*Nephrolepis exaltata* 'Bostoniensis')

Healthy ferns provide an unbeatable lushness with their textured foliage, and nowhere are they happier than in a well-lit bathroom. While they'll want to be kept out of direct sun, they'll thrive with good watering and the damp air. There's a wide range of ferns available, from the lacy fronds of the maidenhair fern (*Adiantum raddianum*) to the bold foliage of the bird's nest fern (*Asplenium nidus*) and the antler-like structure of the staghorn fern (*Platycerium* spp.). However, an easy yet impressive fern to start with, or return to, is the voluminous Boston fern. This fern can grow to enormous proportions and is impressive hung from the ceiling once it's established, with long, draping fronds. However, kept fairly compact, it also makes a great plant to grow on a bathroom floor. Don't let this or other ferns dry out completely, check for watering every few days, especially if it's large for the pot it is in. As well as the higher humidity, your fern will enjoy regular watering but not want to be waterlogged; see pp.86–87 for more advice on how to grow and care for a Boston fern.

If your bathroom has a tiled floor, be careful with your selection of pot to avoid damaging it with anything too hard or rough. Also be aware that anything too soft may wick and absorb moisture from the ground, staying wet. A cover pot made of recycled and recyclable plastic may best suit the damp conditions of a bathroom floor, but if you prefer to avoid plastic altogether and opt for natural materials, just make sure your pots aren't sitting in wet areas and vulnerable to rot.

Any areas of the bathroom, such as the side of a counter or bathtub, can be improved with the addition of ferns. Break up colour schemes and soften edges with the tactile texture of fronds. Your bathroom is the closest room you have to a greenhouse, so enjoy the good light and humid conditions you are likely to have there. Ferns, like orchids, will particularly relish bathroom conditions but are available to buy at a more reasonable price for their size. If you are wanting to create a spa-like environment, add to a collection of smaller and trailing plants with the impact of a large and luxurious fern. Other good spots to grow ferns in the bathroom include the corner of a bath – where there is space for the plant as well its fronds to spread outwards, the side of a sink, or on the windowsill of a frosted glass window.

The Boston fern is one of the easiest and most popular ferns to grow, and it looks fabulous.

Decorate a shadier shelf

Polka dot begonia (*Begonia maculata*)

Not every part of a bathroom will necessarily get good light. Perhaps the room faces the direction getting the least amount of daylight (north in the Northern Hemisphere) or maybe there is an obstruction outside the window that simply prevents much light getting in. Cabinets may cast shade or the room may have an interesting shape, leaving some areas with less light. Or it might just be that the light in the bathroom is absolutely fine for growing in, but you want to grow something in the slightly darker separate toilet instead. Toilets can be wonderful spaces to spruce up with a quirky and interesting plant.

Begonias are great plants for tolerating slightly lower light levels, and on top of the well-known traditional varieties grown for their blooms, there are some wonderful options now sought after for their foliage. *Begonia* 'Rex', known as the painted leaf begonia, comes in a huge array of colours, spiralling out from the centre of each shapely leaf. However, it's the polka dot begonia that has more recently received extra attention due to its incredible angel wing-shaped leaves with red undersides and white polka dots on top. Apart from being wonderfully attractive, its ability to cope with slightly lower light levels makes it appealing and useful for growing in the home. It will thrive in indirect bright light, but its ability to tolerate lower light means it will succeed where some other statement plants will not. Just be sure to avoid very poor light and full sun when choosing a spot for it or any other plant tolerant of low light. It will also enjoy humidity, being originally from the Brazilian rainforests, which makes it a great choice for a bathroom.

If you are growing a polka dot begonia in a small space, keep growth trimmed back, as in favourable conditions it will grow up to a height of around 30cm (12in) to 1m (39in). Alternatively, let it grow up and out, making the most of its glorious foliage and keep it somewhere with more space, such as a sink top or counter. With its elaborate leaves, choose a cover pot that's not patterned or loud in any way that distracts from it. As an upright, structural plant it will complement other smaller leaf or trailing plants such as creeping fig (*Ficus pumila*), which also enjoys higher-than-average humidity and can tolerate some light shade. For more on the polka dot begonia, see pp.116–117.

The polka dot begonia is surprisingly not too fussy for such a beautiful plant.

Embellish a mirror with trailing plants

Silver inch plant (*Tradescantia zebrina*)

While hanging trailing plants saves space and provides a good way to enjoy their shapely dangling foliage, there is scope to get creative with a plant that has a climbing or trailing habit. Use it to your advantage while decorating to soften hard lines in a bathroom by training stems along shelves and around mirrors.

Trailing houseplants can be trained around any mirror. Training over just the top, rather than all the way round makes it easier to keep your plant looking good and attached to the frame. Fastening stems from the underside will require more hooks, spaced more closely together, to compete with gravity pulling the stems and leaves away from the mirror. Of the many options to choose from to train around items in a bathroom (or most other fairly well-lit rooms), the silver inch plant is easy to care for and grows quickly, producing lots of leaves, making it a good plant to use in this way.

You will need to find a way to support the plant and its pot next to the mirror; a compact floating shelf attached to the wall works well, or alternatively keep the pot on the surface below the mirror and trail it up from there. It won't be easy to remove the plant to water it, so make sure it is placed somewhere you can water from a can and isn't too fiddly to check on its moisture level.

To train a trailing plant around a mirror, attach small adhesive hooks or, ideally, adhesive mobile ceiling hanging buttons to the wall just around the mirror itself. You can use plant ties to attach plant stems to the hooks; a hook with a closed circle or eye is easier to tie to without slipping off. Trim back any growth not growing in the direction you want and cut back side growth to keep the remainder bushy.

The stems of the silver inch plant do get leggy as they get older, so start to tie in younger stems as they grow, with a view to cutting out the older stems once they look straggly and the younger stems have established. The deep purple colour of the variegated leaves will look stunning in a bathroom of neutral colours or anything else that complements its dark hue. See pp.120–121 for more information.

The attractive and fast-growing foliage of the silver inch plant makes it a great choice for training around a mirror.

Plant profiles

Once you are familiar with the conditions of each room in your home, and able to work out how the light, temperature and humidity differs in each, you can start getting creative with your selection of plants.

If you want to build a display, you'll have more success growing plants together that thrive under the same conditions. For example, avoid growing big foliage plants alongside succulent plants, since enough light for one will scorch the other, and their watering demands will differ hugely. However, if you're growing plants with the same needs, you can even combine them and enjoy making living arrangements of contrasting and complementing textures and colours.

The much-used phrase, reeled off by many a gardener when making a display of different plants is 'thriller, filler, spiller'. The idea being that you choose your most exciting (and most likely the tallest) plant or plants to grow in the centre, surround them with shorter plants with lots of foliage that cover or fill the area, and finally choose trailing plants to grow around those, spilling out of the side of the container. This is a great starting point when designing your own displays, but ultimately you can arrange your plants however best suits you and your room. You may want to consider the shape of the pot as well as whether the plants will be seen from just one side or more.

The following section of the book offers guidelines in more depth about the care and maintenance of some of the most popular and useful houseplants, with many seen in the previously discussed projects. I have chosen ones that aren't too hard to find in the shops, and only a few are a little tricky to grow.

If you do get a plant that you have no clue how to grow, always start by looking up where the plant is from in the wild. This will help you choose the light, temperature and humidity levels that best match its natural habit. Always use houseplant compost unless the plants are orchids or succulents, for which you can find specific mixes.

For each plant there is a brief introduction and guidance on where in the home to grow it, as well how to do so with success. Also included is a short list of similar plants to try, as well as suggestions of colours that you might consider using around it. The colours have been selected to enhance the natural beauty of the plant and highlight opportunities to integrate the plant with your interior décor. I have looked for both harmonizing and contrasting tones, while also considering which colours simply enhance the appearance of the plant. However, I encourage you to try out different colours; experiment and find the combinations that work for you.

Air plant

(*Tillandsia stricta*)

Quirky

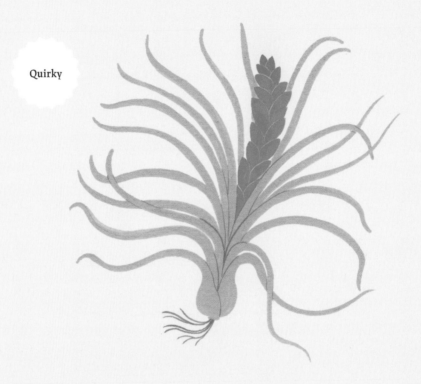

Many similar looking plants are commonly called 'air plants', but this one is easy to find and has a growth habit that suits being placed inside a stand or propped up inside a glass globe terrarium. Originally from the wet tropics of South America and Trinidad, it produces exotic-looking flowers under favourable conditions, which themselves last a few weeks. The plant does die after blooming, but this takes a while to happen. Look out for the new plants (known as pups), that will grow from the base of the plant after it blooms, to grow on. Air plants absorb nutrients and moisture through their leaves; their roots are very few and only used to hold onto surfaces.

Height and spread
Usually around 15cm (6in) tall and 10cm (4in) wide.

Ease of growing plant
(easy)

Suitable light levels
Enjoys bright, indirect light.

Where to grow
These plants love warmth and humidity, which makes bathrooms the perfect spot for them. Kitchens also provide extra humidity, but you'll generally find less in other parts of the house. The solution to growing air plants in a dry room is to grow them inside an open terrarium. This provides a slightly raised humidity but still allows air flow that prevents them from rotting. Don't place the plant on compost as it doesn't need it and will rot. Instead, either keep on a soap dish, in a decorative glass globe terrarium or held in a stand. Stands made especially are available to buy, as are macramé hangers and similar systems to display the plants mid-air. For more ideas on how to display them, see pp.68–69.

How to care
Every week or so give your air plant a soak in tepid water. You can keep rainwater at room temperature to use, providing extra nitrogen and fewer chemicals than in tap water to water the plant, but tap water also works fine. Fill the sink and allow the plant to soak for about 20 minutes, keeping any flowers out of the water as they're fragile. Then shake off gently and allow to drain properly before replacing on display. If possible, allow to drain out upside down, so that there's no water left inside the base of the plant; this will ensure it doesn't rot. Air plants enjoy temperatures around 18–30°C (64–86°F). Frosted windows will suit them as these will diffuse and soften the light.

Colour inspiration for walls, pots and other plants nearby
Turquoise, kiwi green, raspberry pink, pastel red, greyish purple and dark sage are some of the colours that can work well with air plants.

Similar plants to try
- Bulbous air plant (*Tillandsia bulbosa*)
- Sky plant (*Tillandsia ionantha*)
- Xerographic air plant (*Tillandsia xerographica*)

Asparagus fern

(Asparagus setaceus)

Beginner-friendly

This airy plant is neither a fern nor an asparagus, but has attractive foliage and copes better with lower light levels than many other houseplants, making it a very useful choice for difficult spots in the home. The feathery stems of this plant, a relation to the lily, are the reason behind the misleading common name. Left to grow, the stems become more tendril-like and begin to climb, but with regular pruning you can keep it bushy and compact. Native to Southern Africa, this delicate plant has a clean, crisp feel, and will happily grow in a terrarium or out in the open air.

Height and spread
Usually around 50cm (20in) tall and
30cm (12in) wide.

Ease of growing plant
(easy)

Suitable light levels
Enjoys bright, indirect light and tolerates
some low light.

Where to grow
A solution plant for rooms or areas with
lower light levels; try growing the asparagus
fern where others have struggled. The soft,
light texture of the plant makes it a perfect
decoration for a room for relaxation, such as
a bedroom. Kept watered and pruned it also
has a very modern feel, ideal for rooms with
simple and soothing décor. It can produce
flowers, but these are only small and white,
and can be pruned off to retain energy for
new foliage. Cutting back older stems will also
encourage fresh new growth. Any room with
an indoor temperature of around 18–24°C
(64–75°F) and some light will be suitable.

How to care
Avoid growing the plant in places that suffer
from draughts, or above a radiator where it

might dry out in winter, as this plant enjoys
being damp. For foliage that is bushier and a
deeper green, grow in bright indirect light. It
may produce thorns, so watch out for these
when caring for the plant. Reduce watering
in autumn and winter, but don't let it dry out
completely. Snipping back stems will enable
you to shape the plant as you prefer. Remove
dying plant material to keep it looking good.
It will cope with general levels of humidity
in the home, but will enjoy higher humidity.
If you don't grow it in the bathroom, you can
place it there for a few days once in a while
to give it a boost. Houseplant feed can also be
used every few watering sessions throughout
the summer to enhance growth.

**Colour inspiration for walls,
pots and other plants nearby**
Earth brown, light burgundy, dark sand,
parsley green, dark indigo and lavender
purple are some of the colours that can work
well with the asparagus fern.

Similar plants to try
• *Asparagus* 'Myers'
• Blue star fern (*Phlebodium aureum*)
• Cretan brake fern (*Pteris cretica*)

Bird of paradise

(*Strelitzia reginae*)

Showstopper

This eye-catching, statement plant can add real tropical flair to any living space with good daylight. The plant looks contemporary, luxurious and is less commonly grown in homes. Sufficient bright light (generally 4–6 hours) is needed to get a mature plant to produce flowers. However, even if you can't achieve that, the large glossy leaves will grow well in a generally well-lit room and create drama all by themselves. The name refers to the resemblance of the blooms, which are bright orange and blue, to a tropical bird in flight.

Height and spread
Usually around 1m (40in) tall and
60cm (24in) wide.

Ease of growing plant
(medium)

Suitable light levels
Enjoys bright direct light and bright
indirect light.

Where to grow
A bay window or sunny spot on the floor
of a brightly lit room, a kitchen extension
with large windows or a conservatory are
the perfect sites for a bird of paradise. A
south-facing room (if you live in the Northern
Hemisphere) will also work, and like most
houseplants, it will enjoy an extra bit of
humidity. Allow space for the bold, arching
leaves to fall and the majestic flowering spikes
to grow tall. Originally from South Africa,
this plant will cope well with bright light (try
and avoid anything too harsh), but it won't
enjoy draughts. Keep it in a room above 12°C
(54°F), and it will do best at around 18–24°C
(64–75°F). For more ideas on how to display it,
see pp.38–39.

How to care
If you want the plant for its blooms, you will
need to purchase one at least 3–5 years old.

Try to buy one with buds or that is already
in flower to ensure success. Do be aware that
they are sometimes sold with artificial blooms
staked in, so do check you aren't mistaking
something plastic for the real thing. Grow
in a large container, sufficiently weighted
so that the plant won't become top-heavy
and fall over as it grows; you should only
need to repot it every couple of years. Water
generously once a week or so in spring
and summer, and then reduce watering in
winter. Allow the soil to dry out between
watering, but don't leave it to get bone dry.
To encourage flowers, make sure the plant is
somewhere that is cooler in winter, and that it
is kept slightly drier until spring, as this will
allow buds to develop for the following year.

**Colour inspiration for walls,
pots and other plants nearby**
Clear blue, mango orange, wasabi green, pale
orange, light turquoise and sky magenta are
some of the colours that can work well with
the bird of paradise.

Similar plants to try
• Banana plant (*Musa* 'Dwarf Cavendish')
• White bird of paradise (*Strelitzia nicolai*)
• Coconut palm tree (*Cocos nucifera*)

Black velvet elephant ear

(*Alocasia* 'Black Velvet')

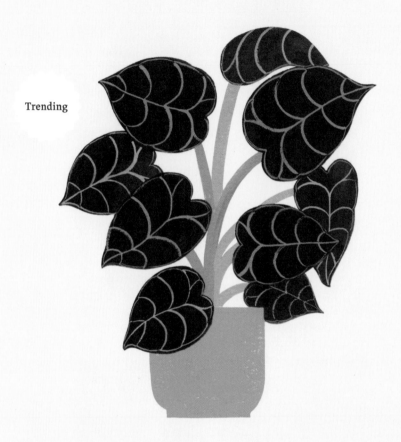

Trending

Smaller than most other alocasias, 'Black Velvet' is slow-growing and will maintain a compact size, making it incredibly useful for adorning a desk or table. The ornate leaves are succulent-like and velvety with contrasting bright pale veins. Sometimes known as a gem or jewel alocasia, this petite but sculptural plant adds elegance and interest to a room. Thought likely to have originated in Borneo, it is best kept away from draughts, but once the temperature and watering are right, it is fairly easy to keep looking smart and healthy.

Height and spread
Usually around 40cm (16in) tall and
25cm (10in) wide.

Ease of growing plant
(medium)

Suitable light levels
Enjoys bright indirect light and some low light.

Where to grow
Any room that stays warm, around 18–24°C
(64–75°F), and is light and draught-free, is
a good spot for this plant. The leaves are
susceptible to scorch, so it's important to
keep it out of sunny spots, but it also won't do
well in very low light. A shelf, table or desk
near a window will provide that bright but
indirect light that so many houseplants enjoy.
As it remains small, it's also the perfect size
to place on a surface that will benefit from
a little pop of intrigue and interest. While it
will enjoy the humidity of a bathroom, if you
want to display it there, make sure you keep it
away from direct light and beware of cold air
coming in from windows that may be opened
suddenly to vent the room. For more ideas on
how to display it, see pp.60–61.

How to care
This plant prefers to be slightly root-bound, so
don't be too eager to repot it – only remove it
from the pot to refresh the growing medium
every few years. As the leaves go over,
prune from the base and look out for brown
tips, which will suggest the plant, or the
air around it, is too dry. In contrast, yellow
leaves may suggest it's too wet. Older leaves
will discolour naturally as they go over so it's
best to check the soil with your fingers every
few days to properly understand how much
moisture there is. It will rot if the soil never
dries out but will also suffer if left too long
between watering. This should be done when
the top layer of soil has dried out, but no
more frequently. Water directly into the pot
avoiding getting the leaves wet and wipe them
dry if they do get damp; water spots may
cause damage to the delicate leaves.

Colour inspiration for walls, pots and other plants nearby
Aubergine, light olive green, evergreen, light
green-grey, dark pastel blue and cashmere are
some of the colours that can work well with a
black velvet elephant ear.

Similar plants to try
- Amazonian elephant ear (*Alocasia* × *amazonica*)
- Hardy elephant ear (*Alocasia wentii*)
- Zebra plant (*Alocasia zebrina*)

Boston fern

(Nephrolepis exaltata 'Bostoniensis')

Beginner-friendly

Ferns are ancient plants that add a fresh, lush feel to any room in the house. The Boston fern is the easiest to look after, and so-called because it is a slight variation of the sword fern that was first sold and distributed from Massachusetts in the late 19th century. It differs from the sword fern in that its long fronds are less upright and have a more arching habit, bending gracefully downwards. With foliage cascading down, it's a popular choice for a hanging basket, but can also be grown on the floor, the edge of a shelf or on a pedestal stand.

Height and spread
Usually around 80cm (31in) tall and 60cm (24in) wide.

Ease of growing plant
(easy)

Suitable light levels
Enjoys bright, direct light and tolerates some low light.

Where to grow
This forgiving and beginner-friendly fern will grow happily in most parts of the house, enjoying a temperature around 18–24°C (64–75°F). However, it will cope with lower light and temperatures as low as 10°C (50°F). For the most luscious and bounciest foliage, grow it in a steamy bathroom. Ensure that it doesn't receive too much direct light, keep it away from draughts or hot air from heaters, and it will grow happily. By rotating the plant every few weeks you'll encourage symmetrical growth all the way around. You can control the size of the plant by trimming back fronds from around the edges; this will also encourage bushier growth. For more ideas on how to display it, see pp.70–71.

How to care
Soak the entire plant every couple of weeks to rehydrate well, then leave to drain out before replacing in its cover pot. This plant recovers well from neglect; if it has dried out, a thorough watering will often bring it back to good health. Test the soil with your finger regularly to assess how dry it is and if it needs watering. Avoid watering too frequently and letting it sit wet. If dark spots develop on the underside of the fronds, these are most likely spores and not pests, so they don't need to be treated or removed. Also, as ferns are non-flowering plants, don't expect blooms. Once a month over the summer, apply a liquid fertilizer if you want to encourage fresh, bright new growth. Fronds can grow nearly 1m (around 3ft) long, so prune to style and cut off any dying foliage from the base of the plant. Repot every other year and be careful not to replant it below the soil level to avoid rotting.

Colour inspiration for walls, pots and other plants nearby
Lime green, lemon grass, deep carmine, sienna, mint and tulip pink are some of the colours that can work well with the Boston fern.

Similar plants to try
- Compact Boston fern (*Nephrolepis exaltata* 'Compacta')
- Maidenhair fern (*Adiantum raddianum*)
- Sword fern (*Nephrolepis exaltata* 'Fluffy Ruffles')

Bunny ears cactus

(*Opuntia microdasys*)

Trending

Native to the Americas, this cactus is a popular choice with houseplant growers. It is known commonly as bunny ears as it develops pads, often in pairs. This unique-looking plant is also adorned with polka dots of fuzz called glochids, which each contain hidden prickles. As long as it is handled with care, this plant is easy to look after and provides contemporary appeal to sunny shelves. It's perfect for spots that are too bright and harsh for other houseplants, enjoying temperatures around 20–36°C (68–97°F). It can be grown alone or in groups and, as with many other cacti, is perfect for using in pots that you don't want hidden under foliage. For more ideas on how to display it, see pp.50–51.

Height and spread
Usually bought at around 30cm (12 in) tall
and 20cm (8in) wide.

Ease of growing plant
(medium)

Suitable light levels
Enjoys bright light.

Where to grow
Sunny windowsills, ideally with south-facing
windows (in the Northern Hemisphere) make
the perfect spot for these arid plants. They
need low humidity, so keep them out of
steamy bathrooms or away from areas that
stay wet. All cacti and other succulents are
vulnerable to rotting if the compost they are
in isn't able to dry out completely between
watering. If you have a plant that is a few
years old and want to encourage it to flower,
move it to a cooler, darker space in the
winter months, no lower than 10°C (50°F),
to encourage the development of buds.

How to care
Temperatures around 20–29°C (68–84°F) are
ideal for bunny ear cacti, but what's really
crucial is getting the watering right. Avoid
watering the pads, but water the compost
thoroughly and let the water drain out.
Ensure the compost mix is a free-draining
cacti and succulent mix, and – as with all
plants – that your inner pot has drainage
holes. Choose a pot that is low and wide
to keep the plant stable, as it may become
top-heavy as it grows. In winter, you won't
want to water more than once a month; the
plant will likely go dormant and want a rest
period. Watch out for splitting pads, this is
a sign of overwatering. Always check the
soil is completely dry before adding water.
To reinvigorate a bunny ears cactus, you
can repot each spring, being careful to wear
protective gloves when handling the plant.

**Colour inspiration for walls,
pots and other plants nearby**
Charcoal, copper, otter brown, swamp green,
oyster pink and sea mist are some of the
colours that can work well with the bunny
ears cactus.

Similar plants to try
• Golden barrel cactus (*Kroenleinia grusonii*)
• Blue cactus (*Pilosocereus azureus*)
• Spiralled cereus (*Cereus* 'Spiralis')

Calamondin orange

(Citrus × macrocarpa)

Luxury

You don't need an orangery to grow a beautiful and fragrant calamondin orange at home. A hybrid between a tangerine and a kumquat, this citrus is the most popular grown as a houseplant as it copes well with the home environment, while producing fragrant flowers as well as tart but edible fruit in summer. The fruit lasts for weeks on the plant and can then be used in cakes and for preserves such as marmalade. There is something almost opulent about an orange tree indoors, and the pop of colour complements many colour schemes, including looking particularly dynamic alongside blue.

Height and spread

Usually bought at around 80cm (32in) tall and 40cm (16in) wide.

Ease of growing plant

(medium)

Suitable light levels

Enjoys bright light and tolerates bright, indirect light.

Where to grow

This dwarf citrus tree can grow up to 3m (10ft) tall, so find a spot where it has the space to grow or prune it each spring to keep it compact. A lover of bright light, it will enjoy rooms with large windows, such as a kitchen, or an adjacent living space. The subtle but sweet and fresh citrusy scent produced by the leaves, as well as the fruit and flowers, also works well in a kitchen environment. As a young plant, it will sit nicely on a kitchen island, table, or dresser. In the winter months ensure it is close to a bright window and rotate it to guarantee each side receives sunlight. The ideal temperature for this orange is 18–24°C (64–75°F) but it will cope with as low as 10°C (50°F) in winter. For more ideas on how to display it, see pp.48–49.

How to care

Check the top layer of soil is dry before watering. You'll likely need to water it more often during the middle of summer.

Use a fertilizer during spring and summer to promote the growth of flowers and fruit. The glossy, oval leaves can be wiped clean every few weeks and prune new growth each spring to keep the plant compact if desired and prevent leggy growth. When pruning, use sharp secateurs and cut just after a leaf on a stem to prevent unsightly die-back. Avoid repotting unless the roots are bursting out of the pot; you'll get more flowers and fruit if the plant's roots are restricted. If you do repot, make sure the stem isn't planted any deeper than it was previously to avoid rotting. The plant won't be naturally pollinated by insects inside the home so use a clean, dry paint brush to wriggle around inside each flower to spread pollen and enable the production of fruit.

Colour inspiration for walls, pots and other plants nearby

Lightning yellow, grenadier red, greenish blue, royal blue, light grey green and peach orange are colours that can work with calamondin orange.

Similar plants to try

- Four seasons lemon tree
  (*Citrus × limon* 'Four Seasons')
- Mandarin orange
  (*Citrus reticulata* 'Clementine')
- Key lime (*Citrus × aurantiifolia*)

Cast iron plant

(*Aspidistra elatior*)

Beginner-friendly

The easiest to keep alive, this is the perfect houseplant for beginners and the shadiest, coolest parts of your home. As its common name suggests, this plant is tough and will tolerate some forgotten watering and less than favourable conditions. Originally from Japan, it was popular with the Victorians who wanted but struggled to grow houseplants in cold, dark spaces with poor air quality. As it's slow-growing it can be expensive to buy at full size, but for those looking for a near-indestructible plant that will cope well in low light, this plant is a true gift.

Height and spread

Usually around 60cm (24in) tall and 50cm (20in) wide.

Ease of growing plant

(easy)

Suitable light levels

Enjoys bright, indirect light and tolerates low light.

Where to grow

Anywhere out of direct bright light works well for this plant; pop it where other plants refuse to grow. Dark hallways, high or low humidity – a cast iron plant will put up with a lot more than other plants can. It will grow well at room temperature, but those already growing outside in the cold will even survive below freezing. Use it to add a flourish of foliage to the corner of a room or space shaded out by large pieces of furniture. Larger plants can be grown on the floor – the classic leaves complement a wide range of pots – while smaller plants can be grown on shelves and tables. For more ideas on how to display it, see pp.34–35.

How to care

The large leaves can collect dust, so do wipe down every few months to keep the plant looking healthy and allow it to properly photosynthesize. It doesn't like to sit in wet soil, so do make sure the compost is nearly dried out before watering; it will prefer to be dry for a while than be too wet. Remember that the shadier the spot it is in, the slower it will dry out. The roots also prefer not to be disturbed, so if you can avoid repotting the plant; only do so every few years once the slow growing plant has outgrown the pot and the compost needs refreshing. An occasional liquid feed in the summer with watering will provide a top-up of nutrients. Mature plants grown in bright, indirect light can produce the odd flower, but these smallish red flowers are insignificant and only sit at soil level.

Colour inspiration for walls, pots and other plants nearby

Olive green, porcelain white, woodland green, maroon oak, royal fuchsia and cement grey are some of the colours that can work well with the cast iron plant.

Other tough plants to try

- Chinese evergreen (*Aglaonema* 'Maria Christina')
- Snake plant (*Dracaena trifasciata*)
- ZZ plant (*Zamioculcas zamiifolia*)

False shamrock

(Oxalis triangularis)

Beginner-
friendly

This eye-catching plant is a fabulous addition to the home as it's both
unusually attractive and very easy to care for. The cluster of deep purple
foliage is made up of three leaflets, each on a stem, and in summer delicate
flowers bloom high above the leaves. In the light, the nearly black foliage is
almost iridescent. The leaves open in the day and close at night and are said
to resemble butterflies on sticks. This plant is robust and will bulk up quickly,
looking lovely on its own or in contrast to other plants with more typical
green foliage.

Height and spread
Usually bought at around 15cm (6in) tall and 15cm (6in) wide.

Ease of growing plant
(easy)

Suitable light levels
Enjoys bright light and bright, indirect light.

Where to grow
False shamrock loves to be on or near a sunny windowsill; it will happily grow in any room with sufficient light and is content with general room humidity. This South American native enjoys a general room temperature of 12–24°C (54–75°F) and as a small plant it works well on shelves. As a larger plant it can be placed on a pedestal stand. It bulks up quickly and you may well be surprised at how soon you have a big plant if growing in favourable conditions. Away from enough light, it will display elongated growth, so move somewhere brighter if this happens and rotate the plant every few weeks to keep the form rounded. For more ideas on how to display it, see pp.62–63.

How to care
Dead foliage and flowers will pull away easily, so rake your fingers through to remove dead material every few weeks. Deadheading will encourage more flowers, so if you enjoy the delicate blooms, keep on top of your maintenance. Water as the compost starts to dry out, reducing this in winter. If there are only a few leaves (or none) in the winter months it's likely that the plant has gone into dormancy, so stop watering and restart once you see new growth emerging in spring or the soil gets desperately dry, then water a little. Unlike most houseplants, false shamrock grows from corms (bulb-like structures), which makes it more forgiving of a few forgotten waterings and will usually regrow when it looks like all is lost. Every few years repot the plant, potting up clumps to give away or moving the entire plant into a bigger pot with fresh compost. Do this in the spring, firm the corms in well and water after repotting.

Colour inspiration for walls, pots and other plants nearby
Slate, greyish green, pastel violet, lavender grey, mercury and hazel green are some of the colours that will work well with false shamrock.

Similarly interesting plants to try
• Red luna (*Peperomia caperata*)
• Rose painted calathea (*Calathea roseopicta* 'Surprise Star')
• Silver inch plant (*Tradescantia zebrina*)

Fiddle-leaf fig

(Ficus lyrata)

Classic
choice

This indoor tree hit peak popularity a few years ago, but is still very much in
favour with interior designers. The combination of large, thick, glossy leaves
on a thin, bare stem creates a sculptural thing of beauty. It also photographs
well, which is why it has such a huge presence on social media and within
the pages of interior design magazines. The name of this West African native
comes from the shape of the large, sturdy leaves, as they are thought
to resemble a violin.

Height and spread
Usually around 1.2m (4ft) tall and
60cm (24in) wide.

Ease of growing plant
(tricky)

Suitable light levels
Enjoys bright, indirect light.

Where to grow
Described as the 'it' plant by *The New York
Times*, this is a glorious and whimsical plant
that will add structure to your home, as
long as you have sufficient light. Placing it
near a window will provide good light, but
you must make sure that it isn't exposed to
draughts. It will grow most happily at 15–25°C
(59–77°F). Maintenance of this plant is low if
the location is right – a sunny living room, or
bright kitchen extension, with big windows
and a skylight will provide the ample sunlight
required. As this plant can grow up to and
beyond 1.8m (6ft), ensure you have space
above it for growth, or prune it back to keep
it at a desired height. For more ideas on how
to display it, see pp.54–55.

How to care
Often bought as a mature plant for its
distinctive structure, getting the maintenance
right is crucial as it is expensive, and you want
to avoid losing it. However, it is possible to find
smaller plants at a more budget-friendly price
in certain large home furnishing stores. Keep
it in a large pot that is heavy enough to stop
it toppling over and only water once the top
layer of soil is dry. When you do water, irrigate
thoroughly and let it drain out. The fiddle-leaf
fig is known to be finicky, so keep an eye on
the leaves, which you can wipe with a damp
cloth to keep glossy. Losing lots of leaves, or if
more than a couple are turning yellow, means
it might be sitting too wet, need watering or
want to be in a sunnier spot. Check the soil
and make sure it isn't too close to a radiator or
any draughts. Top up the compost each year to
add plant food that will slowly seep through to
the roots.

**Colour inspiration for walls,
pots and other plants nearby**
Cucumber green, fern green, cloudy blue,
oyster pink, deep teal and burnt red are some
of the colours that can work well with the
fiddle-leaf fig.

Similar plants to try
• African fig (*Ficus cyathistipula*)
• Rubber fig (*Ficus elastica*)
• Weeping fig (*Ficus benjamina*)

Heart-leaf philodendron

(*Philodendron scandens*)

Problem solver

Heart-shaped leaves tumble down from this trailing plant in abundance, creating a cascade of calming foliage. It's suitable for any room in the house that doesn't receive too much direct sunlight and where it can enjoy temperatures of around 15–24°C (59–75°F). The plant can also be trained to climb up supports; use plant ties to gently attach stems to support and encourage the direction in which you want the plant to grow. Any shelf or ledge at height provides a good spot to grow this plant. From a mantelpiece to a semi-shady windowsill (north- or east-facing in the Northern Hemisphere), this plant will grow happily and soften its surroundings.

Height and spread
Usually bought around 45cm (18in) long and
30cm (12in) wide.

Ease of growing plant
(easy)

Suitable light levels
Enjoys bright, indirect light and tolerates
some low light.

Where to grow
While this plant won't have a problem
growing in any warm room with daylight,
it can be used as a problem-solver for spots
that don't receive enough light for more sun-
loving plants. The casual nature in which the
leaves hang from the plant make it perfect for
decorating a bedroom or a cosy space in the
living room, such as a snug or book corner.
Originally from Central America and the
Caribbean, there is something relaxing about
the way the stems fall if placed to hang from
the ceiling or trail over a shelf or ledge. For
more ideas on how to display it, see pp.42–43.

How to care
Allow the compost in the pot to almost
completely dry out before watering to help
avoid rotting, and then water thoroughly.
Keep the leaves away from direct sunlight to
avoid scorching, and if the plant is grown in

lower light, remember that it will take longer
to dry out. Trim the stems to keep at desired
length and add houseplant feed to water in
the summer every few weeks to encourage
new growth. If leaf tips are going brown,
the air around it may be too dry; while the
plant can cope with average room humidity,
this may be a sign that there is a strong
heat source such as a radiator too close or a
draught nearby. Aerial roots may appear from
stems, and you can take advantage of this by
attaching these stems to a support that you
want them to climb on. If you don't want the
plant to climb, leave the aerial roots alone
and avoid cutting them off as this unnecessary
damage to the plant could cause infection.

**Colour inspiration for walls,
pots and other plants nearby**
Green clay, dusty lavender, Oslo grey, slate
green, light mauve and glacier blue are some
of the colours that can work well with the
heart-leaf philodendron.

Similar plants to try
• Grape ivy (*Cissus alata*)
• Satin pothos (*Scindapsus pictus* 'Argyraeus')
• Sweetheart plant
  (*Philodendron scandens* 'Brasil')

Ivy

(Hedera helix)

Beginner-friendly

Ivy is another treasure of a plant that can be used where conditions are too cold or dark for other plants. This charming, quintessentially English plant is found in abundance outside but can be used to add a touch of the romantic and wild indoors. A vigorous grower, it will trail down bookshelves, climb up supports and is a good choice to use near exterior doors or draughty windows. Small self-adhesive hooks can be used to pin the stems under shelves or up walls. Do be aware that the aerial roots that grow from the stems can mark walls and furniture.

Height and spread
Usually bought at around 15cm (6in) tall and 15cm (6in) wide.

Ease of growing plant
(easy)

Suitable light levels
Enjoys bright, indirect light and tolerates some low light.

Where to grow
Perfect for a shady and cool hallway; avoid anywhere too bright and warm. Native to most of Europe and western Asia, this easy-to-grow houseplant prefers cool rooms, ideally around 10–18°C (50–64°F) and copes well with low levels of light. Use it to fill dim corners and away from too much humidity or hot, dry air. The winding, trailing growth can be trained around mirrors, up wires or hung from hanging baskets. For best growth, provide indirect light, especially for the popular variegated types, which have less chlorophyll in their leaves and therefore require slightly more light to produce energy. For more ideas on how to display it, see pp.32–33.

How to care
Ivy will recover well from some neglect and prefers to be kept drier rather than wet. Keep the soil moist in summer and reduce watering in winter. Check with your finger before watering and try to avoid letting it dry out completely. Prune regularly to keep in the desired shape and length; the speed of growth will depend on how much light the plant gets. It will grow well without fertilizer, but you can add liquid fertilizer to a few of your summer watering sessions to boost growth. Place the entire plant in a bathtub or sink to spray with the shower every few months to remove dust from the leaves and leave to dry before replacing in the desired space. When watering the plant, water thoroughly and then wait for the top layer of soil to dry out before repeat watering. Repot every couple of years to avoid the plant becoming too root-bound; once this happens the plant will dry out much more quickly than before.

Colour inspiration for walls, pots and other plants nearby
Pale taupe, light olive, coral tree, light sea green, atomic tangerine and twilight are some of the colours that can work well with ivy.

Similar plants to try
- Ivy 'Mint Kolibri'
  (*Hedera helix* 'Mint Kolibri')
- Ivy 'Yellow Ripple'
  (*Hedera helix* 'Yellow Ripple')
- Ivy 'Clotted Cream'
  (*Hedera helix* 'Clotted Cream')

Mexican snowball

(*Echeveria elegans*)

Quirky

This pretty and compact succulent plant is perfect for a sunny windowsill, best enjoying bright light and warm temperatures. The plant produces a cluster of leaves that make a rosette, with the leaves looking very much like petals. Even when not in flower, this houseplant provides attractive form for a space too small or bright for other plants. Originally from arid parts of Mexico, as long as it is grown in the correct sandy soil for cacti and succulents, it is an easy plant to keep looking healthy and attractive.

Height and spread
Usually around 20cm (8in) tall and
30cm (12in) wide.

Ease of growing plant
(medium)

Suitable light levels
Enjoys bright light.

Where to grow
Slow growing and compact, this sun-loving
plant should enjoy kitchens, bedrooms,
living rooms and well-lit extensions and
conservatories. Be aware that the humidity
of a bathroom or any dark space won't be
enjoyed by the Mexican snowball and may
lead to rot. If the plant is growing in a room
too dark, it is likely to stretch towards the
light, making it leggy and losing its structure.
Should this happen, cut the rosette of petals
off the elongated stem and repot by placing
on top of slightly moist cacti and succulent
mix, in a sunnier position. It will regrow
new roots; avoid watering until the roots are
firmly established.

How to care
Water occasionally but thoroughly. It is much
easier to recover a succulent plant that is
too dry than too wet. The leaves may look
wrinkled or feel soft when squeezed gently –
this is a sign that it's time to water them, but
do check the soil first. These symptoms could

also mean the plant has stayed too wet for too
long and now is drying out as the roots are
too rotten to absorb moisture. In this case, it
would be best put it somewhere warm with
bright indirect light, where it can dry out
and allow new roots to grow. Avoid getting
water on the leaves and pinch flowers off
once they have gone over; the plant produces
lovely pink, bell-shaped flowers on long stems.
Mexican snowballs grow best in temperatures
around 18–27°C (64–80°F) and certainly
nothing below freezing, which hopefully they
shouldn't experience indoors. Avoid fertilizing
this plant, as it may do more harm than good
to the roots. In the right light and watering
conditions, it should produce small offsets
around the base, which can be left on or
pulled off and repotted.

**Colour inspiration for walls,
pots and other plants nearby**
Faded jade, light sage, watermelon, pink
sherbet, green smoke and pale cerulean are
some of the colours that can work well with
the Mexican snowball.

Similar plants to try
- Burro's tail (*Sedum morganianum* 'Burrito')
- Ghost echeveria (*Echeveria lilacina*)
- Leatherpetal (*Graptopetalum pentandrum*
  subsp. *superbum*)

Mosaic plant

(Fittonia albivenis)

Vibrant

Brightly coloured leaves in vibrant tones of green, pink and red make this plant a stunning and contemporary addition to well-lit rooms of the house. Also known as the nerve plant, the veins of each leaf pop with contrasting colours, making the foliage look almost painted on. In combinations such as neon pink with green, lime green with white, and coral with a golden yellow, each plant bursts with colour, either on its own or grown as a mixed group of different coloured foliage.

Height and spread
Usually around 20cm (8in) tall and
20cm (8in) wide.

Ease of growing plant
(medium)

Suitable light levels
Enjoys bright, indirect light and tolerates
some lower light.

Where to grow
The secret to making this gorgeous, brightly-
coloured plant maintenance-free is by
popping it into a sealed terrarium. Place
the terrarium in any well-lit room with
temperatures around 15–24°C (59–75°F) and
you can almost forget about it. As long as the
plant is firmed well into the soil and watered
before sealing shut, the moisture inside will
keep being recycled and you won't need to
water it. If the glass gets very foggy, move
it to a cooler and slightly shadier spot. For
more information on how to display it inside
a terrarium see pp.40–41. Alternatively, this
plant loves a moist bathroom and with its
petite size and trailing habit, it is perfect for
siting on a shelf away from bright light.

How to care
Originally from the tropical rainforests
of South America, the mosaic plant loves
humidity. Keeping the soil moist and the
leaves away from dry air will encourage strong
growth. Snipping leggy growth will help keep
it bushy, and as the flowers are very small and
not as exciting as the foliage, you may wish
to also snip off buds as they develop. This will
encourage the plant to keep pushing its energy
into producing lush leaves. You can apply
a liquid fertilizer every couple of weeks in
summer to encourage growth. Misting leaves
will temporarily increase humidity, but keeping
the plant in a terrarium or bathroom will help
it grow to be its most perky and glorious.

Colour inspiration for walls,
pots and other plants nearby
Turquoise, seafoam green, cranberry, bone,
soft pink lavender and charcoal grey are some
of the colours that can work well with the
mosaic plant.

Similar plants to try
• *Fittonia* 'White'
• *Fittonia* 'Red Tiger'
• *Fittonia* 'Skeleton'

Moth orchid

(*Phalaenopsis amabilis* 'White')

Classic
choice

Moth orchids are the easiest type of orchids to grow, tolerating a wide
range of conditions in the home. Originally from South-East Asia, they
produce exotic blooms year-round, lasting weeks at a time, and are a
popular choice for interior decorating. Much modern breeding goes into
creating a wide range of varieties these days, however the large and classic
blooms of *Phalaenopsis amabilis* 'White' provide a stunning display that will
complement most spaces. While the colour black is said to be admired by
designers for being both equally arrogant yet modest, a clean and crisp white
must be equally so.

Height and spread
Usually around 50cm (20in) tall and
30cm (12in) wide.

Ease of growing plant
(medium)

Suitable light levels
Enjoys bright, indirect light.

Where to grow
Any room in the house that is around 15–24°C
(59–75°F) and well-lit for much of the day
will suit moth orchids. While they enjoy
higher levels of humidity, they'll cope fine in
a warm and gentle sunny spot in any room of
the house. Direct light, typically that from a
south-facing window in summer for those in
the Northern Hemisphere, may scorch leaves.
However, bright, indirect light will encourage
blooms. In a living room, a coffee table near a
window is a good spot to grow orchids. If space
is limited, miniature varieties offer the option
of a smaller-sized display or the opportunity to
grow a selection together.

How to care
Both full-size and dwarf moth orchids will
require the same care. Let the pots dry out
between watering, with the roots turning a
silver colour to suggest they need water. If the
roots have shrivelled and are flattened, this
indicates that they are too dry and should be
watered more frequently. Submerge the plant
pot into a bucket or sink filled with water for
20 minutes, then allow to drain for the same
amount of time again before placing back
into the cover pots. How often you do this
will depend on the amount of light and heat,
but as a general rule of thumb, do this once
a week in the summer and every 2–3 weeks
in winter. Add a couple of liquid 'bloom' feed
drops into the water (which are high in potash)
every other watering to promote flowering.
Snip flowering stems to just above the next bud
after each bloom goes over. There is no need
to remove the entire stem if still green and
healthy as more buds may develop.

Colour inspiration for walls, pots and other plants nearby
Light teal, dark mauve, tan, pastel red,
lavender grey and dusky purple are some of
the colours that can work well with white
moth orchids.

Similar plants to try
- Mini moth orchids (many varieties available)
- Scented moth orchid 'Miraflore'
  (*Phalaenopsis* 'Miraflore')
- Vibrantly coloured moth orchids, for
  example 'Asian Coral' (*Phalaenopsis* 'Asian
  Coral')

Parlour palm

(Chamaedorea elegans)

Classic choice

This low-maintenance, high-impact palm is a great plant for homes as it provides height, greenery and glamour to many rooms. Native to the rainforests of Southern Mexico and Guatemala, helpfully it is tolerant of a bit of shade and even a little neglect. It can reach up to 2–3m tall (6½–10ft), so do find somewhere that offers space for the plant to grow. It is known as the parlour palm as it was popular with the Victorians, who would adorn their living spaces with them, but with its feathery leaflets and simple elegance it can look attractive in rooms of all styles.

Height and spread
Usually bought about 80cm (31in) tall and 40cm (16in) wide.

Ease of growing plant
(easy)

Suitable light levels
Enjoys bright, indirect light and tolerates some low light.

Where to grow
This handsome plant is best grown against a wall or in the corner of a room to allow it space to grow up and out, as well as not get in the way. It enjoys temperatures around 15–24°C (59–75°F) and the sprays of leaves are almost shrubby and deserve space to fan out attractively. As the plant can tolerate a bit of shade, it doesn't need to be too close to a window, and is perfect for filling a gap in the corner of a room. Providing more height and structure than many houseplants, the popularity of this plant means it is possible to buy large statement specimens that will instantly add impact to your room. For more ideas on how to display it, see pp.58–59.

How to care
Keep an eye on whether the plant is producing new shoots; if not it may need to be moved into a sunnier position if you are hoping for it to grow taller. The parlour plant doesn't enjoy sitting wet, so check the top layer of compost is dry before watering, and check it is not sitting in a pool of water inside its cover pot. Larger plants tend to invite enthusiastic watering, which left unchecked can rot off roots. Use secateurs to cut off any dying stems from the base and add houseplant feed to the watering can every few weeks to encourage growth. If it is getting dusty, move the plant into the shower on occasion and spray the foliage gently to clean. As the top growth is feathery and light, it is a good choice for a plant in a space that you are worried may be knocked over, but keeping the base heavy will further secure it from accidents.

Colour inspiration for walls, pots and other plants nearby
Almond, pastel brown, dove grey, lichen green, pink rose and marzipan are some of the colours that can work well with a parlour palm.

Similar plants to try
• Areca palm (*Dypsis lutescens*)
• Footstool palm (*Saribus rotundifolius*)
• Kentia palm (*Howea forsteriana*)

Peace lily

(*Spathiphyllum wallisii*)

Beginner-friendly

Often seen as a symbol of serenity, this plant is gloriously easy to care for, budget-friendly and complements most styles and décor. Originally from South America and some surrounding areas, it enjoys moist soil, meaning it is harder to overwater, although it is worth lifting the pot to check the plant isn't sitting in a pool of water every now and again. With sufficient light, the peace lily produces elegant and graceful inflorescences – big, white modified leaves, each holding a spike of tiny flowers inside.

Height and spread
Usually around 45cm (18in) tall and
30cm (12in) wide.

Ease of growing plant
(easy)

Suitable light levels
Enjoys bright, indirect light and tolerates
low light levels.

Where to grow
The peace lily can be grown almost anywhere
in the house. Tolerant of shade and low light
levels, it'll flourish in partial light meaning
anywhere out of the harm of direct bright
light, but where it will receive a few hours
of indirect light each day. Kept in low levels
of light it is unlikely to flower, so move into
a brighter spot if this is a problem. Ideally
it enjoys temperatures of around 18–29°C
(64–84°F). While the general humidity of a
room should be fine, look out for brown leaf
tips which can suggest the air is too dry. If
this is the case, move away from draughts or
sources of hot air such as radiators. For more
ideas on how to display it, see pp.30–31.

How to care
What makes the peace lily so easy to care
for is the speed at which it lets you know
it's thirsty. Before any permanent damage is
done, the thin leaves will droop when there is
not enough moisture in the soil. At this point
a thorough watering or soak in a sink will
quickly revive the plant. It can bounce back
from a dry spell more successfully than many
other houseplants. The many leaves can be
kept clean and glossy by being wiped with a
damp cloth every few weeks or a spray in the
shower. It will grow well without plant feed in
a favourable position, but you can encourage
growth by adding a liquid plant feed to your
water every few weeks in spring and summer.
Once flowers go over, snip them and any other
dying leaves off from the base of the plant to
keep it looking smart.

**Colour inspiration for walls,
pots and other plants**
Vivid burgundy, cool blue, steel grey, dark
salmon, potter's clay and iridium are some of
the colours that can work well with a peace lily.

Similar plants to try
• Domino peace lily (*Spathiphyllum* 'Domino')
• Giant peace lily (*Spathiphyllum* 'Sensation')
• Picasso peace lily (*Spathiphyllum* 'Picasso')

Peacock plant

(*Goeppertia orbifolia*)

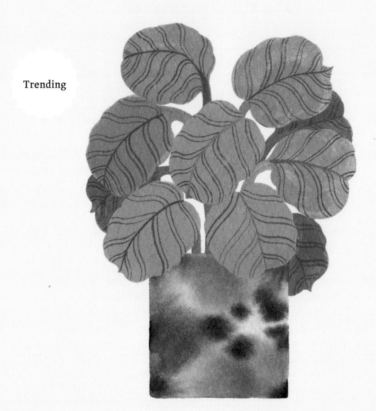

Trending

Originally from the understory of tropical rainforests in Bolivia, the peacock plant (also known as *Calathea orbifolia*) has become a popular statement plant for contemporary styled homes. This may be because the striped markings of the large, rounded leaves are as timeless as a Breton striped top, or that the cool silver grey and cucumber green tones of the glossy leaves make it so appealing. Growing moderately quickly in ideal conditions, it can soon become a decent-sized plant, softening the edges of a wall or adding interest to a room.

Height and spread
Usually up to 1m (39in) tall and about 60cm (24in) wide.

Ease of growing plant
(medium)

Suitable light levels
Enjoys bright, indirect light and tolerates some low light.

Where to grow
A kitchen is the ideal place for this plant, where there is likely to be the availability of good light and protection from direct sun. It will enjoy temperatures around 18–24°C (64–75°F), but will also cope with temperatures as low as 15°C (59°F). It will appreciate the increased humidity levels in a kitchen as well as any light coming from nearby larger windows, external doors or skylights. As it can tolerate some shade, positioning it in a space partially shaded during some of the year should also be fine, just do keep an eye on it. If you want to grow it in a less humid room, such as the living room or a bedroom, watch the leaves for any signs of stress. Where humidity is too low, leaves will start to look shabby. Misting leaves will alleviate the problem, but only temporarily. Keep with a larger group of plants to help create a slightly higher level of humidity around it. See pp.52–53 for suggestions on how to display it.

How to care
As well as doing best in bright but indirect light, the peacock plant also enjoys moist but not constantly wet soil. Check and regulate your watering; you will soon become accustomed to the amount the plant needs over time, but be aware that seasonal changes will alter its needs as the light and temperature levels change. Water the plant thoroughly outside, or in the shower, also giving the leaves a quick rinse every few sessions. Use tepid water when possible to avoid damaging the leaves. Watering thoroughly will ensure that the soil is uniformly wet throughout. Only water again once the top 3cm (approx. 1in) of soil has dried out – this will ensure enough water has left the soil to allow air back into the roots before you re-water and prevent rotting. As the plant has single-leaf stems, just cut each off near the base as they go yellow to keep it looking smart. Rotate the plant every few weeks to encourage symmetrical growth.

Colour inspiration for walls, pots and other plants nearby
Rich lilac, turtle green, light taupe, muted blue, dark mauve and linen white are some of the colours that can work well with a peacock plant.

Similar plants to try
- Maranta (*Maranta leuconeura*)
- Prayer plant (*Calathea veitchiana*)
- Birkin philodendron (*Philodendron* 'White Wave')

Pelargonium

'Best Red'

Classic
choice

Pelargoniums are often misnamed as geraniums. While the two types of
plants are related, the major difference between geraniums and pelargoniums
is that one is hardy and can grow outside year-round (geraniums), while
pelargoniums are tender to colder weather and are better grown as
houseplants in temperate climates or bedding plants in the summer. The
easiest way to tell a pelargonium (which is native to South Africa) from a
geranium is to look at the top two petals. On most pelargoniums these will
appear slightly different from the rest of the petals on the flower.

Height and spread
Approximately 45cm (18in) tall and
35cm (14in) wide.

Ease of growing plant
(easy)

Suitable light levels
Enjoys bright light and bright, indirect light.

Where to grow
Pelargoniums will flower most readily in good
light. 'Best Red' produces strong, uniform
flowers and has vigorous growth when
kept in a bright location. A south- or west-
facing windowsill (for those in the Northern
Hemisphere) will provide ample light. They
best enjoy temperatures around 18–27°C
(64–80°F) and conservatories or kitchens with
big windows can be ideal spots. Do remember
that the more light the plant receives, the
quicker it will dry out. Growing the plant in
a larger pot will slow down drying out times;
however, if you can keep an eye on watering,
growing it in a pot where the roots are tightly
packed will lead to more flowers.

How to care
Keep away from heat sources such as
radiators, which may dry the plant out. As
long as pelargoniums are in a well-lit spot and
not left dry for too long, they are easy to look
after. Do let most of the soil dry out before
watering thoroughly, and apply a houseplant
feed while watering every few weeks during
spring and summer to encourage growth.
A feed high in potassium will encourage
flowers, but snipping off those that have
gone over will also help the plant continue
to bloom. Keep the plant the size and shape
you want by pruning stems back to a leaf
when required, but never more than a third
at a time. Encourage blooms for the following
year by moving into a cooler spot over winter,
which will help it rest (go into dormancy).
Reduce watering to every 3–4 weeks over
winter, checking the soil is drying out, and
you may need to reduce watering further if
it's in a cooler spot. For more ideas on how to
display pelargoniums, see p.62.

Colour inspiration for walls, pots and other plants nearby
Lightning yellow, butterscotch, highland
green, nutmeg, Prussian blue and pale
carmine are some of the colours that can
work well with Pelargonium 'Best Red'.

Similar plants to try
- Geranium 'Attar of Roses' (*Pelargonium capitatum* 'Attar of Roses')
- African geranium (*Pelargonium sidoides*)
- Sweet scent geranium (*Pelargonium graveolens*)

Polka dot begonia

(Begonia maculata)

Trending

With a deep red underside to its leaves, this plant is rumoured to be the inspiration behind Christian Louboutin's iconic red-soled shoes. The polka dot begonia is an incredibly stylish plant that has become popular with many houseplant owners, and is quite unlike any other. Native to the rainforests of south-east Brazil, it is unsurprisingly fond of humidity and warm temperatures. Distinctive splashes of white decorate its contrasting dark leaves, creating a plant that is as much artwork as horticultural pleasure.

Height and spread
Usually around 50cm (20in) tall and 50cm (20in) wide.

Ease of growing plant
(medium)

Suitable light levels
Enjoys bright, indirect light and tolerates some low light.

Where to grow
A well-lit bathroom is the best space to grow this plant, as it thrives on humidity. While it will cope with drier and slightly shadier rooms, it will be at its most healthy and attractive with a frequent boost of moisture from showers or baths. Alternatively, a kitchen will also provide additional humidity, but there is something sensual about this evocative plant that lends itself to a more intimate setting. It enjoys temperatures around 15–24°C (59–75°F) and is easy to keep clipped to a compact size, meaning it will fit nicely on a shelf or above a floor cabinet, adding an exotic and botanical spa feel to your daily rituals. If not cut back and allowed to grow tall, the polka dot begonia can often reach up to at least 1m (3ft) tall and can be grown in an ornamental pot on the floor, beside a bathtub or sink. For more ideas on how to display it, see pp.72–73.

How to care
Once you have your plant in a humid spot, ensure it receives bright but indirect light. The polka dot begonia will tolerate low light but performs best under slightly sunnier conditions. With sufficient light, it will even flower periodically from spring to autumn. However, most people choose the plant for its leaves, so if the little white blooms are not desirable, just snip off to the base of the flowering stem as it develops, diverting more energy into growing new leaves instead. This plant enjoys soil that is moist most of the time but is also allowed a little dry break between watering, so water thoroughly and then wait until the first 3cm (approx. 1in) of soil are dry to the touch before doing so again. If you really want to grow it in a living room or bedroom, group together with other plants to increase the humidity immediately around them.

Colour inspiration for walls, pots and other plants nearby
Peach, deep lavender, medium forest green, eggshell, pale blue and dark sand are some of the colours that can work well with the polka dot begonia.

Similar plants to try
• *Begonia* 'Escargot'
• *Begonia* 'Looking Glass'
• *Begonia* 'Curly Fireflush'

Satin pothos

(*Scindapsus pictus*)

Classic
choice

This is one of the easiest houseplants to grow because it will tolerate a bit of neglect and even slightly lower light levels than many other houseplants, making it is incredibly useful for many spaces. A slow-growing plant native to India and many surrounding areas, it has a trailing habit so is best grown on a wall, hanging from the ceiling or along a shelf. Small, clear plastic hooks can be attached to walls or under shelves to hold onto stems and direct the growth of this attractive plant. The slightly fleshy leaves are ornate and heart-shaped, with variegated green and grey leaves. See pp.28–29 for suggestions on how to display it.

Height and spread
Usually about 20cm (8in) long when bought and 15cm (6in) wide.

Ease of growing plant
(easy)

Suitable light levels
Enjoys bright, indirect light and tolerates low light.

Where to grow
This is a great plant for a tricky area as it will cope well on walls or shelves opposite windows. It doesn't need too much indirect light and will fare better than others in a slightly shady spot. It's surprisingly easy to grow given how striking it looks and will enjoy a general warm room temperature of 15–24°C (59–75°F). Keep away from draughts to keep the leaves looking good and the plant happy. While it won't grow quickly, you can soften edges in any room by training the plant to grow along them. The gentle, whimsical way in which the stems and matte leaves fall provide a peaceful charm to any space.

How to care
The key to caring for this plant is to avoid overwatering it. As with any plant that is succulent and has fleshy leaves, there is a higher risk of the plant rotting. Remember to check that the soil is mostly dry before watering it to avoid this happening. Remove any dead or dying material, either with snips or pull away from the base of the plant. Use a soft sponge or damp cloth to keep leaves clean and use a houseplant feed mixed in with water every few weeks when watering over spring and summer to encourage growth. The flowers it produces are very small and not very interesting so you may prefer to snip these off before they bloom.

Colour inspiration for walls, pots and other plants nearby
Brick orange, rich gold, silk blue, gun smoke, sapphire blue and oyster grey are some of the colours that can work well with satin pothos.

Similar plants to try
• Happy leaf pothos (*Epipremnum aureum* 'Happy Leaf')
• *Scindapsus treubii* 'Dark Form'
• Sterling silver pothos (*Scindapsus treubii* 'Moonlight Care')

Silver inch plant

(*Tradescantia zebrina*)

Beginner-friendly

This eye-catching plant can be trimmed regularly to be kept compact in a pot or allowed to grow and produce long trailing stems that can reach around 2m (6½ft) in length. Native to Mexico and some surrounding areas, it is a versatile, low-maintenance plant, which will add colour and interest to any side table, shelf or space that is too small for larger plants. From the stems hang leaves of purple, green and silver. When the stems are snipped off, it will easily form roots if kept in a pot of soil or vase of water – it's the plant that keeps on giving.

Height and spread
Usually bought about 15cm (6in) tall and 20cm (8in) wide.

Ease of growing plant
(easy)

Suitable light levels
Enjoys bright, indirect light and tolerates low light.

Where to grow
The cascade of colour and metallic foliage will spill over the side of counters, tables and shelves in any room with just a few hours of daylight. The unusual colour combination may suit a smaller room such as a toilet, where it can entertain guests with its quirky appearance, but it will happily grow in most rooms, and average room humidity will suit it fine. In a living room, it can be placed upon a plant stand to create an eye-catching display. Trimming back stems and adding houseplant feed to water once a month will encourage vigorous, shrubby growth. Growing in a well-lit room will also discourage leggy and straggly growth. See pp.74–75 for suggestions on how to display.

How to care
Average room temperatures will suit this plant fine – just don't allow it to grow anywhere that drops below 12°C (54°F). This is one of the easier houseplants to grow and is fast-growing; either cut back to keep compact or repot in spring into a pot that is a size bigger if you want to encourage growth. When watering, check the cover pot to make sure the plant isn't sitting in water. Wilted foliage may suggest the plant is too wet and roots are rotting. If the plant is overwatered, place in a slightly sunnier spot and allow to dry out. Once the plant is starting to recover, over the course of a few weeks cut back the wilted plant stems. This plant can produce flowers, but they are small and not particularly interesting compared to the colourful foliage.

Colour inspiration for walls, pots and other plants nearby
Plum purple, pearl aqua, pastel purple, silver, lipstick pink and deep saffron are some of the colours that can work well with the silver inch plant.

Similar plants to try
- *Tradescantia* 'Green Hill'
- *Tradescantia* 'Nanouk'
- *Tradescantia* 'Sitara'

String of hearts

(Ceropegia woodii)

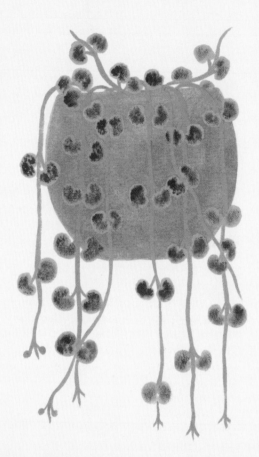

Trending

With heart-shaped, marbled leaves, this houseplant is a lovely addition to a
room. Originally from areas in and around South Africa, it can cope with a
bit of drought but really does need good light. It is worth buying in a shop
rather than online as there are natural variations in the plant; some have
quite a pink tinge to them, which you may or may not prefer. It also produces
small but intriguing pinkish flowers in the summer. This charming plant will
trail its way over shelves and tables, adding greenery to places limited on
height, but with space to cascade down.

Height and spread
Often bought at about 20cm (8in) long and 15cm (6in) wide.

Ease of growing plant
(easy)

Suitable light levels
Enjoys bright light and bright, indirect light.

Where to grow
Tumbling green hearts on thin stems can be draped or weaved anywhere with good light, enjoying temperatures around 15–29°C (59–84°F). On or near a windowsill is a great spot, ideally south- or west-facing (for those in the Northern Hemisphere). It will grow happily for a while in a pot that might seem small for its length. Just a regular 10cm (4in) diameter pot will support the plant as it grows; this means it can be fitted in a small or tight space. Narrow shelves or the space in front of books on a bookcase can work well. Alternatively, you can insert a metal wire into the pot and train the plant to grow in a circular shape by wrapping the stems around it. For more ideas on how to display it, see pp.44–45.

How to care
This succulent plant will forgive you for letting it dry out a bit. It will be much more problematic if you keep it too wet, so be careful with watering. Let the compost dry fully first and do make sure you are growing the string of hearts in houseplant or cacti mix. It may not be sold in compost that is free-draining enough to best suit the plant. If the compost is too moisture retentive, gently empty the plant out of the pot in spring or summer and repot with a more free-draining mix. If you have the plant in a position where you can see inside the pot and spot empty sections on the compost, just move stems across the bare compost and pin into place with a small piece of wire or metal hair pin. The plant will soon produce roots from the stem and grow into the compost.

Colour inspiration for walls, pots and other plants nearby
Greyish teal, dark grey blue, rose gold, pinkish brown, aluminium and bone are some of the colours that can work well with string of hearts.

Similar plants to try
- String of pearls (*Curio rowleyanus*)
- String of bananas (*Senecio radicans*)
- Trailing jade plant (*Peperomia rotundifolia*)

Swiss cheese plant

(*Monstera deliciosa*)

Classic choice

This statement plant has once again become iconic. Having initially been a favourite between the 1950s and 1970s, in recent years it is being seen again in many homes and across social media, particularly in its variegated forms. The shapely leaves and impressive size to which it can grow means it can easily transform a room into a jungle-like oasis. Originally from the tropical forests of southern Mexico, it is easy to find and buy, and is also available at more affordable prices due to its popularity with houseplant owners. The plant is versatile as it will put out aerial roots and therefore can be trained up and around a room.

Height and spread
Usually around 1.2m (4ft) tall and
60cm (24in) wide.

Ease of growing plant
(medium)

Suitable light levels
Enjoys bright, indirect light and tolerates
some lower light.

Where to grow
This is another plant that enjoys a well-lit
room, with bright but indirect light. While
the Swiss cheese plant will welcome a bit of
increased humidity, it will enjoy typical room
temperatures of around 15–24°C (59–75°F) and
tolerate the average humidity of your home.
Choose somewhere near a window to provide
a spot where it can be admired by guests
and have ample space to grow. As your plant
develops, you may want to use a pole or trellis
to provide it with support and direction,
which might influence your choice of space
for the plant. Placing it in the corner of a
room opposite a door will make an impressive
sight as someone enters the room, as well as a
good opportunity for discrete supports to be
propped behind the plant. For more ideas on
how to display it, see pp.64–65.

How to care
This speedy grower will do well in good light
and with attentive watering. Stick your finger
in the pot every week or so; if the top layer
of compost has dried out, remove the plant
from its cover pot and give it a good drink
by watering thoroughly in a sink or outdoors.
If the plant is too big or too much of an
inconvenience to move, water it in place,
stopping when excess water begins to run out
of the holes in the bottom of the inside pot.
Trim off old, damaged or dying leaves from
the point at which they grow from the stem
with secateurs. Move into a sunnier position
if the leaves are not producing their famous
holes, as this will only happen in good light.
As the plant grows, prune to keep in desired
shape and provide a support to cling on to
once you spot it growing roots from the stem.

Colour inspiration for walls,
pots and other plants nearby
Carbon grey, light forest green, bashful pink,
old gold, cherrywood and dark grey blue are
some of the colours that can work well with
the Swiss cheese plant.

Similar plants to try
• Mini Swiss cheese plant (*Monstera adansonii*)
• Oak leaf philodendron (*Ipomoea costellata*)
• Tree philodendron (*Thaumatophyllum bipinnatifidum*)

Watermelon peperomia

(Peperomia argyreia)

Trending

This houseplant is both attractive and easy to care for. Slim flower spikes pop up during the summer but are insignificant and not the reason for this plant's popularity. This South American plant is very much grown for its green and grey striped leaves that resemble the outside of watermelons. The plant provides year-round interest with leaves that are wonderfully large for the size of the plant and remain throughout the seasons. As a semi-succulent, the keys to success are to get watering right and to avoid placing the plant anywhere it may get knocked or brushed as the fleshy leaves are fragile and can easily bruise and fall off.

Height and spread

Usually around 30cm (12in) tall and 30cm (12in) wide.

Ease of growing plant

(easy)

Suitable light levels

Enjoys bright, indirect light.

Where to grow

This is a warmth- and light-loving plant that is best placed out of direct light, but otherwise somewhere as well-lit and comfortably warm as possible, within 15–24°C (59–75°F). It is a compact plant and thus is perfect for desks and tables where other objects like pen pots, picture frames, books or candles sit, or where a screen, mirror or wall-hung picture frame provides limited space below. It can be grown in a group of other plants of a similar size, such as small succulents and cacti, or placed on its own against a plain backdrop to best show off its leaves. It looks particularly pleasing in contemporary settings and works well on a floating shelf as long as it receives good light.

How to care

The leaves of this plant will certainly catch attention in your home, so keep them looking spotless by not getting them wet when watering. Allow most of the compost to dry out before watering and then use a houseplant watering can with a long, thin spout to water directly into the pot around the base of the plant. Avoiding getting water into the base of the plant will also help avoid rot too. Gently wipe the leaves with a damp cloth if necessary and, as the stems are brittle, any dying leaves can be easily snapped off. Average room humidity is fine for this plant, just keep it away from draughts. If the leaf stems seem to be getting too long, this means the leaves are struggling to find light and you should move the plant somewhere brighter. You will only need to repot every few years as it is a slow-grower, and a bit of houseplant feed in the summer months will encourage growth.

Colour inspiration for walls, pots and other plants nearby

Quill grey, pine green, oyster pink, purple taupe, muted blue and burnt pink are some of the colours that can work well with the watermelon peperomia.

Similar plants to try

- Chinese money plant (*Pilea peperomioides*)
- Friendship plant (*Pilea involucrata*)
- Green baby rubber plant (*Peperomia obtusifolia*)

More ideas for growing happy houseplants

Silver inch plant (*Tradescantia zebrina*)

10 additional plants suggested for use in a hallway or other rooms with slightly lower light levels and cooler indoor temperatures:

Chinese evergreen
(*Aglaonema* 'Maria' and other varieties)

Delta maidenhair fern
(*Adiantum raddianum*)

Dragon tree
(*Dracaena marginata*)

Jade plant
(*Crassula ovata*)

Leopard lily
(*Dieffenbachia* 'Green Magic')

Heart-leaf philodendron
(*Philodendron scandens*)

Silver inch plant
(*Tradescantia zebrina*)

Snake plant
(*Dracaena trifasciata*)

Spider plant
(*Chlorophytum comosum*)

ZZ plant
(*Zamioculcas zamiifolia*)

Swiss cheese plant (*Monstera deliciosa*)

10 additional plants suggested for use in a living room or other rooms with indirect bright light and average indoor temperatures:

Angel wing begonia
(Begonia coccinea)

Butterfly plant
(Christia obcordata)

Caladiums
(Caladium bicolor and other varieties)

Christmas cactus
(Schlumbergera bridgesii)

Coleus
(Plectranthus scutellarioides)

Desert rose
(Adenium obesum)

Green velvet alocasia
(Alocasia micholitziana 'Frydek' and other varieties)

Flamingo lily
(Anthurium 'Joli Peach' and other varieties)

Peacock plant
(Calathea orbifolia)

Swiss cheese plant, variegated
(Monstera deliciosa 'Variegata')

Fiddle-leaf Fig *(Ficus lyrata)*

10 additional plants suggested for use in a kitchen, kitchen extension, or other warm and well-lit rooms:

Aloe vera

Basil
(Ocimum basilicum)

**Bolivian rainbow
chilli pepper**
*(Capsicum annuum
'Bolivian Rainbow')*

Coffee plant
(Coffea arabica)

Fiddle-leaf fig
(Ficus lyrata)

Lemon verbena
(Aloysia citrodora)

Makrut lime tree
(Citrus hystrix)

Meyer's lemon
(Citrus × limon 'Meyer')
and other varieties

Miniature rose plant,
many options available

Pineapple mint
(Mentha suaveolens)

Moth orchid *(Phalaenopsis grandiflorum 'White')*

10 additional plants suggested for use in a bedroom
or other warm room with indirect bright light:

Cape primrose
*(Streptocarpus 'Pretty Turtle'
and other varieties)*

Moth orchid
*(Phalaenopsis grandiflorum
'White' and other varieties)*

Chinese money plant
(Pilea peperomioides)

Rabbit foot fern
(Phlebodium aureum)

French lavender
(Lavandula stoechas)

Rosemary
(Salvia officinalis)

Gardenia
(Gardenia jasminoides)

Rubber fig
(Ficus elastica)

Jasmine
(Jasminum officinale)

Weeping fig
(Ficus benjamina)

Peacock plant (*Goeppertia orbifolia*)

10 additional plants suggested for use in a bathroom
or other rooms with higher-than-average humidity:

Blue star fern
(Phlebodium 'Blue Star')

Coconut palm tree
(Cocos nucifera)

Fishtail palm
(Caryota mitis)

Guzmania bromeliads
*(Guzmania 'Hope' and
other cultivars)*

Lipstick plant
(Aeschynanthus radicans)

Living moss wall art

Peacock plant
(Goeppertia orbifolia)

Orchid 'Apollon'
*(Dendrobium 'Apollon' and
other cultivars)*

Sweetheart hoya
(Hoya obovata var. kerrii)

Wax plant
(Hoya carnosa)

Watermelon peperomia (*Peperomia argyreia*)

10 suggestions of unusual
plants as gifts for houseplant lovers:

Carrion flower
(Stapelia orbea)

Jewel Orchid
(Macodes petola)

Coffee plant
(Coffea arabica)

Marimo moss ball
(Aegagropila linnaei)

Desert Rose
(Adenium obesum)

Sensitive plant
(Mimosa pudica)

Dwarf umbrella tree
(Schefflera arboricola)

Venus fly trap
(Dionaea muscipula)

Ficus Bonsai tree
(Ficus retusa)

Watermelon peperomia
(Peperomia argyreia)

Further reading

For information on plant toxicity see the Horticultural Trades Association (HTA) website: **hta.org.uk/poisonousplants**

Books

Here are a few of the many good books available to take a look at next. Where possible authors' Instagram handles have been included.

Allaway, Zia and Fran Bailey, *RHS Practical Houseplant Book: Choose the Best, Display Creatively, Nurture and Care, 175 Plant Profiles*, DK (2018) @ziaallaway

Camilleri, Lauren and Sophia Kaplan, *Bloom: Flowering plants for indoors and balconies*, Smith Street Books (2022) @leaf_supply

Carter, Hilton, *Wild Interiors: Beautiful plants in beautiful spaces*, CICO Books (2020) @hiltoncarter

Cheng, Darryl, *The New Plant Parent: Develop Your Green Thumb and Care for Your House-Plant Family*, Abrams Image (2019) @houseplantjournal

Doane, Morgan and Erin Harding, *How to Raise a Plant: and Make it Love You Back*, Laurence King Publishing (2018) @houseplantclub

Domoney, David, *My Houseplant Changed My Life: Green Wellbeing for the Great Indoors*, DK (2021) @daviddomoney

Durber, Sarah, *Make Your Own Indoor Garden: How to Fill Your Home with Low Maintenance Greenery*, White Owl (2021)

Gerrard-Jones, Sarah, *The Plant Rescuer: The book your houseplants want you to read*, Bloomsbury Publishing (2022) @theplantrescuer

Horwood, Catherine, *Potted History: How Houseplants Took Over Our Homes*, Pimpernel Press (2020)

Langton, Caro and Rose Ray, *Root, Nurture, Grow: The Essential Guide to Propagating and Sharing Houseplants*, Quadrille Publishing Ltd (2018) @studio.roco

Le-Britton, Tony, *Not Another Jungle, Comprehensive Care for Extraordinary Houseplants*, DK (2023) @notanotherjungle

Leon, Gynelle, *Plant: Houseplants, choosing, styling, caring*, Mitchell Beazley (2021) @prickldn

Maguire, Kay, *The Kew Gardener's Companion to Growing Houseplants: The art and science to grow your own houseplants*, White Lion Publishing (2019)

Peerless, Veronica, *How Not to Kill Your Houseplant: Survival Tips for the Horticulturally Challenged*, DK (2017) @veronicapeerless

Ramstedt, Frida, *The Interior Design Handbook*, Particular Books (2020) @trendenser

Ratinon, Claire, *How to Grow Your Dinner: Without Leaving the House*, Laurence King Publishing (2020)

RHS The Little Book of Cacti & Succulents: The complete guide to choosing, growing and displaying, Mitchell Beazley (2022)

Sibley, Emma, *The Little Book of House Plants and Other Greenery*, Quadrille Publishing Ltd (2018) @londonterrariums

Sparke, Penny, *Nature Inside: Plants and Flowers in the Modern Interior*, Yale University Press (2021)

Vincent, Alice, *How to Grow Stuff: Easy, no-stress gardening for beginners*, Ebury Press (2017) @noughticulture

Watson-Smyth, Kate, *Mad About the House: How to decorate your home with style*, Pavilion Books (2018) @mad_about_the_house

Instagram
Find some suggested profiles below for online inspiration and advice, but do also check out the suppliers and authors listed on Instagram for further advice and ideas.

@blackgirlswithgardens
Both indoor and outdoor plant advice, a resource providing representation, support and inspiration.

@houseplantplantclub
San Francisco-based houseplant blogger.

@idrinkandigrowthings
Houseplant tips from Chicago-based grower.

@jamies_jungle
UK-based green home décor advice.

@mr_plantgeek
UK-based inspiration and advice.

@oneproudplantmama
Sharing photos from the online houseplant community.

@pengsucculents
Succulent specialist and RHS medal winner.

@plantkween
A Brooklyn-based non-binary houseplant collector sharing entertaining tips and advice.

@soiledplanties
Houseplant inspiration and advice on care.

@succulentcity
Focused on the cacti and succulent community.

@thegardensofgaia
Inspiration and guidance.

@thejungalow
Houseplant lifestyle brand.

@thepottedjungle
San Diego plant collector with a love for all things design.

@ukhouseplants
Plant advice provided for hundreds of plants.

@urbanjungleblog
Igor Josifovic and Judith De Graaff provide design-inspired inspiration.

@urbanjungling
Plant care and styling advice.

Podcasts
BBC Gardeners' World Magazine podcast. Episodes – 'Houseplant success with Hilton Carter' and 'Growing Cacti with Gynelle Leon' – presented and interviewed by me.

Bloom and Grow Radio – interviews with houseplant experts.

Gardening with the RHS – advice and ideas from the Royal Horticultural Society. Episode – 'Houseplant takeover!'

Home of Houseplants – Interviews with houseplant collectors across Australia.

In Defence of Plants – In-depth look at plants, including ones grown indoors, exploring the world of botany.

On the Ledge – UK-based show addressing plant problems and ideas for growing.

Plant Daddy Podcast – Growing advice including Q&As.

The Houseplant Coach – Podcast addressing the less common houseplant problems.

Suppliers

Below is a list of some of the many places where you can buy houseplants, pots and accessories. Areas for delivery are subject to change and include limitations of regions. Check each website's shipping policy before ordering to ensure they will deliver to your specific area.

Worldwide
Etsy.com
Ikea.com

Europe
bloomboxclub.com
lovetillys.co.uk (air plants)
theplantcorner.com
wildernisamsterdam.nl

UK
beardsanddaisies.co.uk
conservatoryarchives.co.uk
craftyplants.co.uk (air plants)
dobbies.com
forest.london
happyhouseplants.co.uk
hortology.co.uk
jarandfern.co.uk (terrarium kits)
n1gardencentre.co.uk
patchplants.com
petershamnurseries.com
prickldn.com
thelittlebotanical.com
thenunheadgardener.com (London)
thestem.co.uk

USA
logees.com
pistilsnursery.com
rooseveltspdx.com (terrarium kits)
thesill.com
thingsbyhc.com (accessories)

Australia
leaf-supply.com
thegoodplantco.com.au
thehouseplantshop.com.au
foliahouse.com.au (Melbourne)

New Zealand
theplantproject.co.nz
thenode.co.nz
Planthouse.co.nz

Glossary of useful terms

Below are some terms that you may find useful or helpful for houseplant shopping and further research.

Activated charcoal
Charcoal that has been treated at a high temperature. Some growers add this to their growing mix to absorb toxins and improve drainage, among other benefits.

Aerial root
A root growing above the ground. Plants may grow just these, none, or as well as roots in the ground. The production of aerial roots can sometimes indicate a problem with the roots inside the growing mix.

Cachepot
Another term for a decorative outer pot or cover pot. It won't have drainage holes, so mustn't be planted into directly.

Coir
Coconut fibre that is used in growing mediums, sometimes as a component in peat-free alternatives.

Dormancy
Some plants and seeds have a period of rest or do not respond until certain environmental triggers happen, such as light and temperature levels.

Inflorescence
A single or group of flowers on a stem. Sometimes what looks like one flower is in fact a collection of many.

LECA
'Lightweight expanded clay aggregate' are baked clay balls that are sometimes added to growing mixes for plants. The clay absorbs moisture, releasing it slowly while also providing extra drainage in the growing medium.

Medium
The growing mix that plants are grown in. This can range from a single component to a mix of many ingredients.

NPK
Nitrogen (N), phosphorus (P) and potassium (K) are the three macro-nutrients in most balanced plant feed. You will often see a ratio on a plant feed labels that explains how much of each is inside.

Offsets
Small but complete plants that have naturally grown on the parent plant. These can usually be removed and grown separately once mature enough. Spider plants are famously good at creating these, also known as 'pups'.

Propagation
The process of creating new plants from parent plants. This ranges from growing seeds to taking cuttings and many other methods.

Pumice
Volcanic rock sometimes added to growing mediums to improve drainage.

Rootbound
A plant that has grown too big for its pot will often have roots that grow in spirals as they search for space and nutrients. Also known as 'pot bound'.

Rooting hormone
Applied to plant cuttings to encourage the development of roots in order to produce new plants, usually in powder form.

Vermiculite
Volcanic glass that is added to growing mediums for improved drainage, aeration and soil structure. It is also sometimes used to help germinate seeds.

Index

This book is dedicated to Lily Elizabeth Luke, my greatest love.
May you always be inspired and delighted by plants.

Acknowledgements

This book is made possible by the wonderful support around me. Many thanks to Tina Persaud for commissioning this book, as well as those at Batsford Books for helping create yet another beautiful publication. Nicola Newman, Kristy Richardson, Frida Green, Gemma Doyle, among others – it is a huge pleasure to work with you again.

Georgie Mcausland (@georgiemcausland) has created the beautiful illustrations, spinning my rough sketches into works of beauty – absolute magic, and for this I am very grateful. Francesca Herrick kindly provided her assistance with proof-reading, and for this I thank you greatly.

Thanks are due to all of those who taught me how to grow houseplants at the Royal Botanic Gardens, Kew – Paul Rees, Bala Kompalli, Rebecca Hilgenhof, Scott Taylor, Elisa Biondi and Andrew Luke (whom I took away with me). Plus, many more horticultural staff and the very knowledgeable minds also working in the Herbarium.

The De Beauvoir Gardeners have continued to support me since I started training in botanical horticulture, right up until the present day, and for their love and support I am very grateful. The team at *BBC Gardeners' World Magazine* also continue to offer wonderful support, and kindly allow me to juggle the incredible work we do with my own publications.

Many thanks are also due to my wonderful friends for keeping me going. These include, Alex Casey, Anna Gibson, Anne Blood Mann, Brigid McFall, Delia Edwards, Donna Hume, Emma Curley, Kelly Brodie, Rita Cottone, Shiraz Mehra and Vienna Rae, plus many more and the amazing mums of Leighton Buzzard. I am also grateful to the help from Richard Harryman, who took the time to help me understand the financial side of becoming an author.

I cannot mention all my relatives who have been supportive, as in particular my Irish side is exceptionally big, but the level of support has been surprisingly high. This has amazed me and touched my heart – I thank you all greatly and love you dearly. But huge thanks must go in particular to my mother, Brigid Doyle, whose love, encouragement, and support is endless – I am incredibly grateful.

Of course, to the previously mentioned Andrew Luke, my partner and father to Lily Luke, I am grateful to you both for all your love and support. Finally, but not lastly, to Henry, my canine ride or die; you are also very loved and appreciated... just not by my houseplants.